BASEBALL KARMA
& The Constitution Blues

BY

Ronnie Norpel

ISBN: 978-0-692-21364-3

Printed in the United States of America
Text set in Bembo Regular

Published by
AD LIB PUB, New York

www.constitutionblues.blogspot.com

For My Mom

and

All Ye Hometown Fans

"I don't know if it's you guys [the media] or the players or what, but somebody out there has got something against us. Or somebody's not living right. If you guys are very religious, please go to church. Pray for us."

—Charlie Manuel—
Phillies Manager
July 7, 2006

Luck is the residue of design.
—Branch Rickey—

Failure is the true test of greatness.
—Herman Melville—

GAME

Let me make the superstitions of a nation and I care not who makes its laws or its songs either.

—Mark Twain—

Lucky Chucks, Wishbones & Making the Team

Sometimes we must wait until enough people are dead to tell a story. Other times we must tell a story before more people die. The lie implied: telling stories—especially tales out of school, can get you in real trouble. Get ya labeled a muckraking nut. If there's an omerta involved, fuggedaboutit. Then again, if we all went back to confession, we could put Jerry Springer out of business: redeem our culture, recover our lost souls and refortify our collective constitution.

My name is Mary Katharine Carmichael, my R.I.P. list is getting too long, now hear my confession: some twenty years ago, I put a curse on my hometown baseball team. I never thought it would stick, but an intractable vapor lock grips the club to this day. Short of calling an exorcist, I figure the quickest way back to baseball heaven is to tell.

I grew up in St. Genesius parish, an Irish Catholic ghetto in suburban Constitution, where the boys played Little League and the girls twirled batons. I would have preferred

Little League, or at least working the snack bar. I heard those snappy snack girls used to sneak behind the CISCO'S STEAKS billboard on the left field fence and smooch anyone, just to see what first base was like. Maybe then I would have been better prepared when I got called to the bigs.

⚾ ⚾ ⚾

THE DAY WAS BLUE-SKY CRISP, late March a score ago. Pop and Uncle Frank were over for the usual Sunday dinner, which visit, as usual, began Sunday afternoon. Uncle Pat received special dispensation to escape his parish duties, so he came too. We would surprise Pop with a cake for him and my little brother Denny after dinner. But first, Pop hit the Barcalounger with his crossword puzzle and tuned in the Constitution Blues game, while the unks took over the backyard with us kids.

Wiffleball was the game of choice those Sunday afternoons. Baby-in-the-Air was too every man for himself, and Ditch It was best played after dark.

I stood in, swinging my brown ponytail. I swatted the air with the trim yellow stick, and sassed my Uncle Frank.

"We want a pitcher, not a belly itcher!" I took his first pitch.

"No batta, no batta, no batterrrr!" My brother Joe yelled from third. Though he was just fourteen months older and we had three sisters younger, he always introduced me as his "little" sister. Probably to keep the guys away.

"This is your big chance, Mick Carmichael!" Uncle Frank started his wind up. "Don't blow it!"

Uncle Frank was the one who christened me "Mick" when I was born, telling my parents I needed a cool nickname: "It's short for the M-K of her proper name," he explained to my mom—"proper," of course, referencing the Baptismal.

Our neighbor Nelson gave it his gangly greasy best from second base.

"Ah, she's a GIRL! Of course she'll blow it!" His eyebrows looked like flattened shag carpeting. His sexist dig only made me want it more. If there was one thing I couldn't stand, it was guys who thought they were better than me for the mere fact they were guys.

Uncle Frank threw. I smashed a fly over Nelson's head to right-center. I trotted the bases, waving thank you thank you to my imaginary fans, was embraced and high-fived by my teammates Trish, Maggie and Tom, and touched home. I pivoted on the plate and smirked at Joe and Nelson, cross-armed in centerfield, before running in the back door. I got your girl right hee-yah, yo.

⚾ ⚾ ⚾

A HUGE DINING TABLE TOOK up most of our kitchen. A garage sale cross inscribed "Bless This House" hung above the back door. Pop's preseason ballgame chimed from the den. I strutted in the back door and flashed a Victory V at my mom, who was in the final throes of dinner prep.

Mary née Meehan, in her politically active career, had fed her brood Romaine instead of iceberg lettuce to honor the United Farm Workers, likewise un-Quikening our milk when N-E-S-T-L-E-S was reported to be pushing formula over the breast in the "Third World," whatever that was. Atop her jewelry box on the doilied dresser next to the Blessed Mother statue sat a curved steel bracelet engraved "1-22-73: *Roe v. Wade*." Further, she refused use of the Kenmore, because she wanted there to be enough water for her *grand*children: we kids ranged just 5 to 12 when she started her 'no dishwasher' kick, and we giggled at the idea of having kids of our own. But Mom penciled the boys into the KP rotation, and we girls "got to" mow the lawn—saving my brothers' future wives chore-splitting headaches and affirming us girls our equal stake-ownership of the half-acre playing field out back, life itself.

Mom flashed a V back at me.

"You're a winner, kid. Could you do me a favor and set the table? Thanks, I counted twelve." Twelve may sound like a lot of people, but with seven of us kids, Mom was always cooking anyway, so what were a couple more mouths? Extended family and friends often stopped by—"for justa cuppa." She was in fact a better listener than chef.

I peeked my head around the door jamb of the trophy-filled family room, rushed in and kissed my Pop hello. First Communion, Confirmation, Little League, soccer and other team photos lined the paneled walls. The most famous of bronzed artifacts, Dad's "Chucks," were angled just so on the bookshelf next to Tom's Catholic League Championship trophy. Tom and the Irish Mafia (Ward, O'Keefe, Coogan, McKeever, Kane, Dwyer . . .) had played their hearts out when Dad wore his bobos to their football games, going undefeated for St. Genesius grade school. Legend has it Popeye Lawn, St. Gen's stentorian Sunday lector (and father of Tom's best bud, Harry—who would show up in Hollywood years later)—Popeye Lawn made Dad rush home pre-coin toss when he mistakenly arrived for the final contest in Docksiders instead of his knock-off All-Stars.

I kissed my Pop.

"Hey, Pop, what's the score?" I didn't care that much, but he loved the Blues and supposedly the team was going to be good that year.

"They stink!" If it always made him grumpy, why did he watch?

"You think they're bad, you should smell Joe's sneakers."

It had been a treat when a few years earlier Pop had taken us all out to buy new sneakers. I got the red-striped Adidas called Viennas. I loved them.

Pop and I shared a chuckle over my poke at Joe. I loved Pop, and he loved me, and that was just it. I was his eldest granddaughter, but we had an odd bond beyond that, starting when I was twelve and broke my leg on a roof-jumping dare. I thought my life was over, no more beating the boys in foot races; but Pop had *lost* part of his leg at twelve crossing his bike over the tracks in South Constitution, so what was I complaining about? And my dad had been hit by a car at six, his little foot crushed by the lumbering DeSoto; as kids we would wonder at the rectangular ditch-scar on the back of his leg where smooth skin had been stolen to patch his instep. My roof-jumping failure and subsequent trauma seemed preordained—on both sides of my family tree.

"Look at these bums!" said Pop. "Five-zip!"

Uncle Frank and Uncle Pat, now wearing a Roman Collar, entered the den and sat down to watch. I passed to the china closet, atop which sat the heirloom replica of the Pietà, and counted out the good silver.

"No sense getting worked up over it, Dad, it's just spring training. Nice pitch."

I turned and looked at the TV.

"Besides," continued Uncle Frank, "it's a loooong season." We all looked expectantly at the TV.

On the screen, the pitcher finally threw again—a ball.

"One and one," said Glenn Goodall, the Constitution Blues' play-by-play guy. The catcher Moss Thorne tossed the ball back and squatted for the next pitch, idly scooped the dirt behind home plate, lifted his mask and spat. "There are permanent chaw stains behind the plate down here at Dambreau Field after all Moss's years with the Blues."

The pitcher looked in for Thorne's sign.

"At the rate this guy's pitching, it *will* be a long season," I said. But I stayed. The Blues' team character was defined by its lack of pitching, year in, year out. Dearth would be more like it—a dearth of pitching. Like death with an r. "OK, now, don't forget to adjust your e*quip*ment."

On the screen, the pitcher scratched himself.

The unks looked at me. I laughed. I had watched enough baseball to know certain patterns: take sign from catcher/ scratch/wind-up was standard for pitchers.

"There ya go! Throw the ball already."

The pitcher threw. I turned to my uncles.

"How can you sit here and watch this?"

"Strike. Atta boy," said Pop, not paying me any mind. He knew I loved this stuff—I just hadn't watched enough. We waited for the next pitch.

"It's a little deeper than wiffleball, Mick," said Uncle Frank. "They've been playing it for over a hundred years."

"Yeah, you have to have patience to be*come* a baseball fan," said Uncle Pat. He made it sound like the priesthood.

You see, Uncle Pat had been as a seminarian called to the Catholic bigs—a scholarship to the North American College, in Vatican City. When it was time, Pop flew his flock, including my parents, to Rome for Pat's ordination "by Pope Paul VI himself." Even at age four, I could sense this was important— hardly an honor more blessed than being turned into a priest by the Pope. I tried to stay brave for my younger sisters while we were left at St. Stephen's Orphanage. Mom's Aunt Greta made the arrangements with her old friend Sister Sophia who was in charge there, and Pop made a generous contribution for our three week stay. Who else could manage four young children for that length of time? They were sure we would have fun with the other kids. But Joe had to stay separately in the boys' dorm.

Mom yelled from the kitchen.

"OK, everybody, five minutes to show time, wash your hands!"

Uncle Pat stayed on his soapbox.

"You have to give it more than a quick five minutes if you're ever going to appreciate the beauty and timelessness of the game."

"Oh, Uncle Pat, you've been reading too much Tom Bosley," I joked.

Even though Uncle Pat was a priest, he was a cool priest. He knew from The Fonz, and read books and traveled all over and brought us souvenirs. He once gave me a Disneyland coloring book, boy, did that grab me: Frontierland, Adventureland, Tomorrowland—I was ready! I certainly felt it was a Small World, between all my relatives and the people who knew us. In Constitution, you didn't ask, "What section of the city are you from?" Too many words. "What parish ya from?" did it for us.

Uncle Frank shouted at the TV.

"AH, shit!"

"And 'e struck 'eem out," said Glenn Goodall.

Our heads all snapped to Uncle Frank, who bashfully smiled back.

"Excuse me." He turned to me. "Bos-well."

"An-gell!" I just loved teasing Uncle Frank. I was pretty sure he got that reference, at least. I exited the family room, silver in hand.

My siblings flew in the back door and raced past the table, grabbing slices of cucumber from the salad and stealing rolls from the basket on the way through the kitchen. Despite the swarm, Mom continued her dinner sashay: oven and fridge doors are opened, closed, opened, closed.

I set the table, finishing just as the room refilled. Everyone took his place—Dad at one head, Pop caned his way to the other—and we joined clean hands for grace. All heads bowed.

"Thank you, Lord, for the many gifts you have given us, especially the gift of life. God bless the birthday 'boys'," Dad said, looking at Pop, who nodded at him, and then little Denny, who danced in his chair, "and keep us all in your care as we move through our lives this week. Amen."

We prayed at home, as well as at church. At bedtime when we were little, we would recite specific names: "Aunt Patsy's brother Davey McMulligan, Father Forster's cousin Pete, the Dougherty's nephew Kenny," then add, "and for all the boys in Vietnam," then Mom would cross our foreheads in turn: "God bless you."

Everyone answered variously "Amen," "God bless the cook!" and "Birthday boys!"

"And, God bless the Blues for Pop!" I added, winking at him.

"They're gonna need all the help they can get," Pop said. "I'll take that wishbone when the turkey's clean." Pop always took the wishbone. I wondered whether he took them all to Mass, maybe to get blessed, stuff does get in your bones.

We passed the serving dishes, filled our plates and began eating. Maggie, my second sister piped up. She was always piping up.

"Hey, Pop, maybe Mick can play for the Blues? She won the game for us today." Maggie grinned ha ha at Joe.

"Shut up, Mags." Joe hated to lose. "Besides, Uncle Frank threw it."

Uncle Frank shrugged.

I smiled at him and nudged Trish's foot under the table.

We Carmichael sisters were tight and cherished every opportunity to remind Joe and all our boy friends that girls could do anything, beat the boys at ball or even be President of the United States if we wanted to. The chores of home-making stole most of Mom's time, but we recognized her all-around smarts and capability, and she instilled us with self-competence, and a twist-and-shout anthem by Helen Reddy. We pretty much knew we were invincible.

Trish nodded "we're the best" across the table at me. Joe's relentless teasing having cowed her, Trish left the kid-ding to me and Maggie. We happily took up the slack on her behalf.

I got up and started clearing the table.

"Mick, I wanted some more potatoes, Sweets," Pop said. He loved his sweet potatoes.

"Yes, Miss Mary Mick, what's the rush?" asked Dad as I continued to clear the table.

"Sorry," I answered, "I'm due at Pattersons at 6, and I don't want to miss the singing. The faster we clear the table . . . " Pop gave me The Look.

"Don't worry, I've done my homework." Pop had worked hard all his life, filling in for his absent alcoholic father, for his alcoholic mother and three brothers. Aunt Greta went into the convent and became a teacher. So we had this family will toward hard work and studying, and Pop wouldn't let me forget it. Nonetheless, he seemed to accept my one sentence reply. I'm thinking he knew where Mrs. Patterson worked, so he let it go.

Maggie and Trish got up to help me clear.

Mom placed the candles on the cake at the counter, then centered the cake on the table. Gesturing at the unusual can-dle arrangement, she said, "We've got an eleven . . . and a seventy-one." Two columns of four blue candles each formed the 11, with three white candles in a row at the top of the left blue column forming the top of the 7 in the 71.

I turned out the lights, and four year old Chris clapped with glee. Maggie and Trish returned to their places at the table.

We began the song. "Happy Birthday to you, happy birthday to you, happy birthday, dear Pop and Dennn-ny! Happy birthday to you!"

Denny and Pop leaned in to blow out the candles, and I yelled, "Make a wish!" and snapped a picture.

⚾ ⚾ ⚾

I HUSTLED DOWN THE STREET to the Pattersons.' I passed the overgrown yard fronting the peeling lime paint of my child-hood friend Angela's old house. I glanced at the faded lamp-post nameplate: MORRONE, and my eyes fell to the sidewalk. I hated those guys for making fun of her name, and obvious puns are boring besides. I continued my jog-walk down the street and turned up the Pattersons' driveway.

Carol and George Patterson had studied for their son's Baptism at St. Genesius with my mom. Joe was their first sitter, but he tired of it. I liked sitting for them. They paid well and had good snacks. My mom would never stock Doritos and Oreos.

Plus, Mrs. Patterson worked for the Blues, and once she gave me a pair of tickets, but I had a big test the next day, so my dad met Uncle Pat down at Liberty Stadium for the game. I figured maybe I'd get to go another time.

I stepped up to ring, and the door swung open. Mrs. Patterson, a sharp brunette with friendly eyes, nodded and hurried to the car with a briefcase slung over her shoulder.

"Mick, prompt as usual, thanks. The boys are fed, their pajamas are on their beds, and 8:00 is lights out."

I nodded and picked up the baby.

"See you."

Mrs. Patterson added, "You're the boss! I won't be very late!"

Backing out of the driveway, she waved to me and her boys, the tot beside me waving back, holding my hand with his other.

⚾ ⚾ ⚾

I AWAKENED TO KEYS IN the front door. I shook my head clear, my eyes coming into focus on the TV, the late news.

"The Blues dropped their Mango League contest this afternoon," said Constitution's favorite sportscaster Peter Pace, as Mrs. Patterson came in.

"Mick, you want a summer job?"

I popped off the couch, plumping the pillows to erase the spot where my body had become embedded.

"Sorry, Mrs. Patterson, I must have dozed off," I said, not quite hearing her question.

She handed me some papers.

"Take a look at these," she said, "and bring them down tomorrow night if you're interested."

I glanced at the papers, and my heart stopped. Then started beating really fast.

"I know you'd enjoy it." Mrs. Patterson took my Montgomery Lacrosse jacket from the closet and put it around my shoulders, walking me toward the door.

"Thanks a lot, Mrs. Patterson!" I said a little too loudly.

Mrs. Patterson shushed me and opened the door. I walked out and started up the street. She called after me softly.

"And, call me Carol."

I turned around and yelled back.

"Your boys were really good tonight!"

A neighbor's front light went out.

I lowered my voice to a stage whisper. "Carol."

I dashed up the street, I had it made! All except convincing my parents to let me take the job. But, how could they say no? And Pop was just gonna die!

ESP, Psychocybernetics
& Ballpark Figures

Walking to school in my lacrosse uniform on Monday, I decided to keep my own counsel until I got my first shift under my belt that night.

I had a terrible crush on my Honors English teacher, Harris Winkle. I realized he was an odd choice, he was a foot shorter than I and looked like a Russian spy, so I didn't really have a *crush* crush on him, I just liked his thing, his interests. I was in love with his mind.

Mr. Winkle instilled passion for stories in the morning, then went home and wrote—sometimes novels of clairvoyants locating missing people, other times today's fresh handout entitled: "The Great Girl Syndrome?"

I read on about how "Great Girls always do their best, but if their best ain't good enough in time, they will accept a zero rather than offer less than their actual, untimed best." Great, just great. Great Girl Syndrome—ha!

Though Harris's attention was a secret inspirational thrill, I had asked him not to use my work on class handouts. I was tired of being held up as an example, and the crush amplified my embarrassment. My whole life Mom would remind me of my duty to "set a good example for your younger brothers and sisters." I possessed such a habit of doing the right thing that—on their contrived instinct—adults put me on some kind of pedestal. I certainly didn't buy into it. On the other hand, I loathed the idea of disappointing anyone.

What Harris didn't know was how teetery my pedestal was—I hadn't written a single word for him! I was so busted. My imagination the night before had run in every direction except his Glasnost assignment.

Mrs. Patterson had hooked me up with the chance of a lifetime, and I was going to make the best of it. I pictured it all: I might be starting as a Blue Belle, but I thought if I were really good, worked hard and paid attention, well, heck, someday I would own the team! That would be fun.

So I skipped the assignment, and Harris couldn't resist teasing me about it. You might think he had a crush on me too. Or maybe he was right. The difference between lay and lie would be the rare grammar on which his Great Girl would ever trip. But that's a stadium-sized gap when you're heading to the majors with no life experience.

⚾ ⚾ ⚾

In the cafeteria, a group of senior girls leaned in at the back table. Gossip was not really my speed, but I spotted Donna's red lax jersey in the mix and gave her the hi sign.

Barbie, the well-developed know-it-all, held Donna, Kimberly and the others rapt.

"Spike told me himself. If you think about it, it's not surprising. I mean, look at her mother."

Girls with older sisters act like they know more than the rest of us. I *was* the older sister: despite my straight A's, I didn't know shit. Maggie knew way more about life than I did. For all I didn't know, she had already lost her virginity.

I put my tray down next to Kimberly.

"Whose mother?"

"Angela Morrone's," whispered Donna across the table.

"What about her?" I said.

Barbie seemed almost annoyed, "You know, isn't she a drunk?"

I shrugged.

"They left my neighborhood. I never really see Mrs. Morrone around anymore."

"Exactly," Barbie sniffed, nodding at the other girls.

"What are you talking about?" Now it was my turn to get annoyed. Barbie was such a busty bitch, but at the time I was too nice to have thought her anything more than a jerk. Maybe I was the jerk.

"Let's just say Angel's in trouble," Kimberly offered.

I screwed up my face, impatient with Kimberly's vagueness. Donna answered my look.

"Like, fallen."

I knew this was not just another broken-legged dare. Spike must have finally "convinced" Angela. I sighed and quickly changed the subject. I had let Ang go when they lost the house and moved away. All I could do in my guilt was end the inquisition and hope she would be OK. I took a magazine off the table and held it up.

"What the heck is this goofy-looking blue thing?"

"Hey, that's mine!" said Kimberly, grabbing the fresh Constitution Blues yearbook back from me. "That's the Bluesman, our new mascot, and inside are my boys."

"*Your* boys?"

The others cracked up. It was beyond established fact that Kimberly bled Constitution Blue. Her father had had Sunday season tickets for centuries, or at least forever.

"Yeah, myyy boys!"

I clasped my hands in prayer toward the book, and Kimberly handed it back to me.

"The home opener's tonight! I can't wait to see 'em, especially Jack and The Gunner."

Kimberly always used the players' nicknames like she actually knew them, or even owned the team or something. I found that annoying—especially since the night before I had concocted my own plan to own the team someday.

"'Jack' and 'The Gunner'?" I leafed through the book to the player profiles—lots of off-season hunting and fishing, not many philatelists. There was Homerun Champ Jack Black, jersey number 21, of course, and Ace Pitcher Tommy "Gunn" Gunninski, number 1. The Blues had a third outright future Hall of Famer in catcher Moss Thorne, #22.

"Well, my Pop said Gunn's the best he's ever seen, and he's been following them way longer than you, Kim!"

I recognized Mark Ridley, the relief pitcher from yesterday's game. Suddenly, I wanted to—needed to—read the book cover to cover. I fell in, flipped a few more pages: all time team records, last year's stats, family photos, longest Liberty Stadium homers; then stopped at the funny looking rookies, Doug Akins and Bobby Bahnson.

The rookies always look a little retarded in their stiff new hats.

The class bell rang, and Kimberly grabbed the yearbook from me as the other girls walked out.

"Better eat up, Mick!"

I wrapped a roll and a brownie into a napkin, stashed them in my book bag, and hurried out behind Kimberly, wondering how much she might hate me the next day.

OUR PSYCHOLOGY TEACHER DISCUSSED ESP. I secretly felt I had a touch of precognition, but I didn't talk about it—or my obsessive reading of my horoscope. I had been advised that fortune telling was against the Catholic religion—right up there with pre-marital sex and birth control—so I kept my foggy notions to myself.

Not including cartoon cutie Speed Racer, my first serious crush was at nine on Pat the paperboy with his delivery of news from the outside world, including the horoscopes. But first, I would check the box on the lower left front page of *The Almanack* detailing the running "Crime Count" for the year in Constitution:

Robberies:	45
Burglaries:	126
Homicides:	23
Rapes:	11

One day, I asked Mom what rape was; I recognized the other transgressions.

"Rape," Mom explained emotionlessly, "is when a man forces himself upon a woman and has sexual intercourse with her against her will."

Wow, I thought, why would a man do that if intercourse was for people who were married? This sounded awful, so I stopped reading the Crime Count.

The good news was on the inside of *The Almanack*: the glamorous adventures of Brenda Starr and her asterisked eyelashes, and the daily horoscope, in my case, Cancer. I would bask in the front stoop's late afternoon sun, waiting for Pat, moon at him a moment, then dash inside and flip to the predictions.

One time, my horoscope said something about "scrubbing the floors." That very night I spilled turpentine in the tiled basement, and spent the duration scraping up the brown clay formerly known as linoleum with the help of our baby sitter—another Cancer, of course! I was convinced this chemical reaction had been preordained and became a bigger horoscope fan than ever.

My sign's Cancer-Moon Child discrepancy bugged me. I had seen both terms used, and I much preferred "Moon Child" to "Cancer," because my Gram had been taken by the big C. On the other hand, avoiding use of the word *cancer*, especially in an unorthodox practice such as astrology, smacks of superstition, and superstition is definitely prohibited by the Church.

⚾ ⚾ ⚾

THE CATHOLIC ENCYCLOPEDIA HOLDS THAT "Superstition is the baseless fear of the gods, religion the pious worship . . . Superstition sins by *excess* of religion, and this differs from the vice of irreligion, which sins by *defect*. The theological virtue of religion stands midway between the two." [†]

Idolatry is the specific superstitious practice of "inordinate veneration for human excellence" caused by the "influence of demons who offered themselves as objects of worship to erring men . . . doing things which to men seemed marvellous." Other sins of superstition occur when "meaningless elements are added to the approved performance" of religious worship, or supernatural powers for good or evil are attributed to causes "evidently incapable of producing the expected effects."

But what then of Chinese fortune cookies, Bazooka Joe comics, and the full Indian on the Tootsie Roll wrapper? And how to reconcile those dueling talismans of your faith: Aunt Mary's rosary and Mickey Mantle's rookie card? You see, baseball is a superstitionist's minefield, marvellous idolatry and approved performances be damned.

Ritual to the nth degree can turn control into superstition, whether in church or at the yard. You instinctively dip and bless yourself with Holy Water when entering or leaving church, and avoid the baseline heading on and off the field. Yet you find, when you forget, and step on instead of over the line, your subconscious has been wed to superstition in a faithless ceremony meant to drive the spooks away. After transgressing fate, it's just a matter of time until it comes back and bites you on the ass. And so we supplicate.

⚾ ⚾ ⚾

I BOARDED THE TEAM BUS after Psych and massaged the lucky penny on my lacrosse kilt to amp the good karma. I had found the penny on the walk home after the first day of practice and soldered a mini-safety pin on its back. I wore my homemade penny pin on my uniform every game, and it had taken us to a 5-2-2 record—on its back? Well, why not? (Psych!)

⚾ ⚾ ⚾

JOE AND NELSON APPROACHED THE Jaspertown lacrosse field. I took a pass from Donna, cradled past the defender, and scored a goal—my third—to seal our victory. Donna and I hugged as the referee blew the game-ending whistle.

Joe yelled and waved.

"Mick!"

I looked over and raised my crosse, walked to the team bench and dug my duffle from beneath it.

"Great game. See ya tomorrow, Don."

"Where you in such a rush to go with those guys, Mickster?"

I smiled a secret smile.

"Oh, they're just giving me a lift. See ya tomorrow." I'm outta here!

I squeezed into the front seat of Nelson's pride & joy Impala between the guys. We pulled out in front of the team bus and headed downtown to Constitution.

"'Oh, they're just giving me a lift.' Likely story, Mick!" Joe laughed at my white lying to Donna. "I'll tell you, though, Mom said it's given Pop a real lift, he's calling everybody, telling them you're working for 'the bums.'"

"Yeah, but it's not like I can get in the line-up and make a difference in the team's chances or anything. It's really just a job . . ."

Nelson and Joe started laughing: I had to be kidding, they knew I was bursting!

"That's not to say it won't be fun . . . " I opened my bag and began alternately applying make-up in the rearview mirror and munching on my now stale lunch roll.

Nelson always had his radio tuned to WZRD-FM, Constitution's home of Southern Rock. We all jammed.

"What's your name, little girl?! What's your name?! Shouldn't ya stay, little girl, where there ain't no shame?"

"Mick, it's 'Shootin ya straight . . . won't ya do the same!'" It was Joe's pleasure to correct me. I liked my lyrics better.

"That's such a great tune," Nelson said. "Bummer their plane crashed." He merged the Impala into the Freedom Expressway's rush hour traffic. "Speaking of jocks, you know they named their band after their gym teacher, Leonard Skinner?"

⚾ ⚾ ⚾

Our beloved elementary gym teacher, Mike Cooke, had set me on the road to jockhood beyond neighborhood games and climbing the backyard tree to scope the Devereaux Mansion atop Montgomery Hill. "Cookie" had medicine balls and parachutes and scooters. And his annual Gym Awards.

As a third grader who had only that winter transferred from Catholic school ("A gym class, what's a gym class? Yay! Gym class!"), I watched in reverence the bestowing of the Gym Awards at the year-end assembly. Fourth, fifth and six graders in the spring performed a series of ten fitness tests; points accumulated, the top four finishers of each gender per grade earned Cookie's gold-sealed certificates.

In fourth grade, I didn't know the games well enough to be award-level competitive. The shuttle run was the worst— a stupid timed test running between and grabbing and balancing two bowling pins. What the heck kind of test was that?

Fifth grade was an exciting year. The hip Miss Rosenberg was our very own private Rhoda. With her we recycled newspapers into Earth Day field trip dollars and put on plays. Thanks to Miss R's gender-blind casting, I ruled as King Arthur when we did "Connecticut Yankee."

As spring neared that year, I began Gym Award preparation weeks ahead, running sprints with my sisters in the backyard. They were not yet old enough to compete for an award, but I convinced them it would be good practice for them too, that good example thing. The 50-yard dash was approximately one length of the yard; to practice the 100-yard dash, then, we had to make a turn, which added many unfortunate seconds to the "real" time. I guessed I did OK that year, but Cookie never gave out scores except for the top four—again the usual suspects: Peggy McCabe, Andrea

Schomstein, Gloria Dorigio and Josie Jones. I had one more shot the next year. I had to do it.

Two particular skills converged to help my sixth grade cause. First, my math skill: I finally did the math, and realized that more chin-ups was the answer, each one being worth 1000 points. Maximizing chin-ups would be the quickest way to gain points. In fourth grade I had done one chin-up, and in fifth grade two, barely. Though my biceps weren't bad, my wrists were twiglets. I started practicing chin-ups on my dad's closet rod.

The second skill which aided my quest was one which until that time I had not yet harnessed: the power of my mind. I had picked up Mom's self-help paperback, *Psycho-Cybernetics*, and eaten it for lunch. It had lots of great ideas for a sixth grader with Gym Award lust to digest:

> *"Mental pictures offer us an opportunity to 'practice' new traits and attitudes, which otherwise we could not do . . . If we picture ourselves performing in a certain manner, it is nearly the same as the actual performance. Mental practice helps to make perfect."* [†]

I put the book's suggestions to work, visualizing myself doing chin-ups. I rode my bike thinking of chin-ups, I cut the lawn doing chin-ups. In my spare moments, I did mind chin-ups. Then, on the day of the chin-up contest, I did five chin-ups—just enough. I loved gym class almost as much as getting the award, especially pleased to have earned it through working out my brain as well as my tomboy brawn.

⚾ ⚾ ⚾

NELSON GOT US DOWN TO South Constitution in thirty minutes. Liberty Stadium, here I come!

"So, I'll meet you by Gate C after the game. Mrs. Patterson, I mean Carol, said that's where the locker room is," I told them, mascara brush to lashes. The Impala dipped into a pothole. "Nelson, please don't swerve!"

"Calm down, Mick. Everything's going to be fine after your lobotomy," Joe said. "It's cool you're working for the Blues and all, but be careful."

"Did you say 'locker room?'" Nelson wagged his shaggy brows.

⚾ ⚾ ⚾

I STOOD OUT IN MY red plaid lacrosse kilt when I entered the locker room: a lively flock of blue hotpants. The Blue Belles, the corps who greet 'em and seat 'em at every home game, are like stadium stewardesses. Most are 18-35 years old—except for a couple three hold outs from the days at Sheehan Park, the Blues' original home. I smiled bashfully at a few of my new teammates, then spotted Carol Patterson at her desk in the far corner. I walked over and handed her my application.

"Hi, Mrs. Patterson, I made it! We won, 5-3! Joe and Nelson drove me down here as soon as the game ended."

Carol winked at me.

"Hello, Mick, here's your uniform. You'd better change, gates open in T-minus five."

I waded through the blue to an empty locker and began my transformation from athlete to usherette. I unlaced my dusty cleats, toweled the dirt splotches off my calves, and sniffed my armpits. Whew, thank God I brought Mom's Secret! I heard laughter behind me and turned.

A manicured black gal sat at a picnic table in the center of the room, snacking and smoking, while her loud friend wearing a "Debbie" nametag applied lip gloss. These two were surely veteran Blue Belles. I could tell just by looking at them that I had a lot to learn before I could ever own the team. I gave them a weak smile and turned back to my locker.

The black girl leaned in.

"Who's Little Red . . . ?"

"Obviously a virgin, Jacqui," said Debbie. "Not to mention a brown-noser."

Jacqui and Debbie snickered.

I pulled on the uniform, a Parrish blue polyester top and shorts combo bearing the team's bell logo on the left breast. I was comforted by the familiar ritual of suiting up before a game.

The idea behind pre-game routines is to over-control the Ordinary in anticipation of handling the Extraordinary. Just as Einstein's daily "uniform" of white shirtsleeves and black trousers dispensed with the Ordinary, availing his mind of the Extraordinary, so batting champ Larry Walker's uniform number 33 paced his playing days: he would set his alarm for 3 past the hour, shower at the 3rd nozzle, and take 3 swings before each at-bat. Their embroidered vestments elevate our big leaguers to priestly status, even as they superstitiously covet their own jersey numbers: Mr. Clemens thought his 21 worth a Rolex, and Rickey H gave Turner Ward 25G for 24. (While John Kruk accepted two cases of brew from Mitch Williams for 29.) Culinary habits are also controlled: Wade Boggs ate chicken before every game. From arriving at the yard at the same time and parking in the same spot every day to wearing the same dirty jockstrap, if that's what the Church of Baseball dictates, these guys'll do it. On faith.

⚾ ⚾ ⚾

THE ZIP-FRONT ONE-PIECE STYLING OF my new uniform reminded me of the red, white and blue-flowered outfit

I got for my tenth birthday and loved. That was the summer of Hurricane Arthur and the Jonesville flood: the backyard was a swamp, no ball for weeks except hours of jacks on the kitchen floor. I prayed for days before that it at least not rain on my birthday. We hoped ever again to see the sun. The day I turned ten, not only did it not rain, the sun played peek-a-boo. Ah, the power of prayer!

I looked at the blue bell logo over my heart and thought of Pop. He was so pleased and proud I'd gotten the job. I really wasn't that big a Blues fan, but this job definitely beat baby sitting, those older girls' looks notwithstanding.

I pulled the white patent leather boots over my stockinged feet, right—zip, then left—zip, and stood up. I wasn't sure about the boots. They didn't feel that practical to walk in, let alone up and down stairs, and weren't particularly sporty. I got a crazy flashback: Joe using his brown art projector to blow up a nudie, his charcoaled rendering of which I could replicate to this day. (I studied it like other kids would a Playboy pin-up: the low curve of the downstage breast versus the pointy-nippled upstage offering.) And then there was our parents' reaction to this image having been rendered by my brother: an inordinate, muffled confusion of No-ness. No, that's not right, Trix aren't for Kids after all. Least not 'til they're married.

OK, but that wasn't me, and that wasn't here, this was a sports environment, white go-go boots aside. And the uniform matched my eyes. And, it had that logo identifying me as a member of the team: The Constitution Blues. Cool!

Carol Patterson raised her voice from the corner of the room.

"Listen up, Belles! A friendly reminder for everyone, veterans included—you must stay at your section unless you are on break—no wandering around . . . "

I exchanged looks with the girl beside me. At the table Jacqui and Debbie rolled their eyes as Carol continued.

" . . . We are a professional organization, and Mr. Preston feels that the gametime personnel set the tone for the fans. He has a powerful pair of binoculars and is on constant watch from his box, so be advised . . . And, remember: fraternizing with the players is grounds for immediate dismissal!"

I saw Jacqui and Debbie make scary faces at each other. They stood up, and gathered their snack trash.

The Belles filed out of the locker room in small chatty clusters, a few stragglers stopping at the bulletin board to re-check their section assignments. I turned to the girl beside me.

"Fraternizing?"

"Didn't you hear her talk about special gametime assignments and team promotions during initiation?" the girl replied.

"No. I, uh, missed initiation," I said.

"How'dja pull that one off, rookie?" the girl said.

I hesitated, then looked directly into the other girl's eyes.

"Well . . . I'm Mrs. Patterson's baby sitter. She offered me the job, um, yesterday. I haven't been to Liberty Stadium since the opener four years ago with my uncle's softball team." What the heck, it was the truth.

"Wow, you're really in! Mr. Dunbar—head of security —is my neighbor, but I still had to come to the Lib for an interview."

"Please don't tell any of the other girls." I looked over toward the picnic table. "I didn't realize the competition was so, um—fierce."

I felt like I had entered a secret universe with its own traditions and rules, a special argot all its own. The last thing I'd want anyone to think was that I had slid in on someone else's merits or that I had been given special treatment.

"Your rep's safe with me, Sis! I'm Kelly Green." She extended her right hand. I shook it firmly.

"With a name like that, you must be Irish. Carmichael, 'Sister' Mary Katharine. My friends call me Mick. You Catholic too?"

"Just finishing up at West. Hopefully no real nuns will spot me here before graduation!" Kelly laughed at her own joke. I wasn't sure what made it funny, which made me a bit nervous.

"Go to it, ladies!" Carol's voice echoed over to the bulletin board area.

We noticed the empty locker room and hurried out. It wouldn't be right to get in trouble with Carol, after all.

I headed to my section, 338, third level, inside third base. I looked down the aisle at the field: star-spangled bunting draping the baseline fences, freshly swept AstroTurf with its emblazoned blue bell logo, paint smell wafting up from the visiting dugout's "ATLANTIC LEAGUE" designation. The Lib. I didn't remember Liberty Stadium ever looking this dressed up—but, of course, it's Opening Night!

I managed Section 338 with the help of an early arrival, a season ticket holding, life long Blues fan named Chuck. Chuck explained that the section is actually the front half of the one with your number, plus the back half of the section prior. I thus seated my slice of the full house at my first home opener as a Constitution Blue Belle half in 336, half in 338.

The PA announcer, Duke Braun, greeted the fans from the field as they filled the park, and warned them about cans, bottles and ground rule doubles.

If a fan touches a ball which has crossed the baseline after passing the first or third base bag and before being touched by a player, the hit is declared a ground rule double, which rule works to the home team's advantage or dis-, depending on which team is batting. But many fans just can't *not* touch the ball as it veers their way, no matter the situational base-runners. This lesson can be one of the hardest: either way, the fan is summarily ejected, usually televised, often embarrassed.

Duke Braun announced the opponents' lineup: lots of booing and hissing from the crowd, which I found a bit rude.

But when the homers hear: "Starting at second base, and batting leadoff for your Constitution Blues, Number 6, Phill Watson," all hell breaks loose. But it's a good kind of hell, like heavenly hell. The roar draws me in.

Braun worked the fans' excitement through the Blues line-up:

"Batting second, Number 19, the third baseman, Tim Schlitz . . . " followed by, "Number 13, in Centerfield, Doug Akins . . . Number 21 at First Base, Jack Black . . . Number 35, Rightfielder, Andres Lopez . . . Number 22, your Catcher, Moss Thorne . . ."

Oooo—lots of whistling and cat-calling when Thorne was announced! He had a hard ass reputation, and the South Constitutioners couldn't get enough of him. Spike his own mother going into second, that guy.

Duke Braun kept the fans revved.

"Number 8, at Shortstop, Jimmy Simons . . . Number 17, Leftfielder, Bart Hudson . . . and the starting pitcher, Number 1, Tom Gunninski." All call and response, Braun moderating his timing to the fans' cheering.

"Go, Gunner!" "Go, Tommy!" "Go, Blues!" The fans were psyched; so was I.

Duke directed the crowd's attention to the neon bell atop the high bleachers in centerfield, where "Kiteman" stood by in his thunderbolt costume.

The plan for Kiteman to hang-glide across the Lib was the team owner's latest Opening Day stunt. Lloyd Preston was notorious for pulling the wackiest promotions in the 70s, including:

Sunday Sunday Sundae—After a Sunday game in July, a lucky group of fans was selected to stay for Ice Scream With The Team. Ice cream sundaes were served—after fans 'served' cream pies to their favorite players!

Old Rag Day—Fans got a free ticket for every 20 pounds of old newspapers they brought in for recycling; bonus team caps were given to fans whose papers were all the *Daily View*, the city's sports "rag."

Christmas in July—The Bluesman would dress up as Santa, and fan ticket numbers were called for gifts. Top prizes included skis, lift tickets for area resorts, and a weekend in the nearby Managawna Mountains. Game tickets were half-price for fans bringing an old winter coat for Good Will.

Girlfriends Day—Women could buy tickets 2-for-1, and hotdogs were not served. (OK, maybe not.)

⚾ ⚾ ⚾

KITEMAN GLIDED FROM THE TOP of Liberty Stadium, over centerfield, and landed on home plate, holding the First Ball aloft. The fans went wild. I clapped too and felt the crowd's electricity surge through my body. I was amazed to be a part of it. The fans' home team spirit evoked the evangelical prayer meetings I attended when I was in junior high: an itchy commitment solidified when surrounded by fellow believers.

Man is by his constitution a religious animal.[†] The Church of Baseball is a particularly American sect with its homespun saints. The field is the altar, where all the action takes place. The altar batboy genuflects off to the side, looking forward to his day in The Show, while the youngsters in the bleacher-pews watch the batboy's every move, wanting to be him, saying those prayers.

I stood proudly erect for the National Anthem, singing along as I would ever after. Feeling my future ownership vast in front of me, I strained the last phrase: " . . . and the home—of the—brrrraave!" (Years later I laughed to learn that the game's Processional Hymn was originally the popular theme song for an organization of upscale London boozers, the Anacreonitic Society, c. 1760, Anacreon being the ancient Greek poet known for his songs of women and wine. One man's Star-Spangled Banner is another man's checkered past.)

Sporting his beat up glove on his right paw, Geator McFarley, the retired hero of the only Series the Blues had ever won, stepped to the mound. You could not hear Duke Braun announce him, the fans were so nuts. Geator waved to his public, then turned a pirouette on the rubber, pointed his right foot tight beside his left calf, lifted his arms high above his head, arched back, and threw his trademark screwball to Moss Thorne for the ceremonial first pitch, a strike.

And the fans went insane. And my rookie season began.

⚾ ⚾ ⚾

"PEANUTS, GET YOUR PEANUTS HERE!" A female peanut vendor, what do you know? She wore a Blues cap over her tousled brown curls, big framed glasses and bones. And that voice!

"Peaaa-nuts!" As the vendor smiled her way up my aisle, I noticed the miniature peanut, hanging from a gold chain around her neck like a First Communion cross. The Church of Baseball—and peanuts and Cracker Jack.

Tom Gunninski took the mound, the fielders took their positions, the batter stepped in, the first pitch was thrown, and the game was on!

The fans were all so nice to me, it was as if they were the greeters and I their guest. I remembered the Bluesman from Kim's yearbook as I watched his mid-inning dugout dance: he was funny-looking, true, but he was actually funny too.

The choreographed rituals continued. The priests make the Sign of the Cross to start the next play: x marks the spot in the batter's box dirt, the third base coach gives his blessing across his shirt. Pass the plate, time for the collection, the squeeze is on.

The Bluesman suddenly appeared and bounded up my aisle! At the top of the staircase, the mascot grabbed me, tossed me back and put his fuzzy, smelly snout right in my face. Yes, smelly.

Under my squeals, I heard, "Hey, cutie, you're cute!"

"Huh?" I said. His voice sounded cute. Wow! The Bluesman live, up close and personal, jumping off the yearbook cover into my first game!

"Gotta go!" He took off on his motortrike, which one of the Liberty ground crew had pulled up behind my section.

I waved a stunned good-bye.

Chuck was up the aisle in an instant.

"Kissed by the Bluesman! You know what that means, don't you, Mick?"

"C'mon, Chuck, I just got here, remember? No, I don't know what it means."

Chuck didn't know what it meant either, in fact it "meant" nothing, to be kissed by the Bluesman, he was really just kidding; but at this point, he didn't want to let down the cute new Blue Belle: it means I wish I could kiss you.

"It means you're going to marry a ballplayer!" Chuck announced.

I looked at him like he was crazy and felt myself blush. The idea of marrying a ballplayer had never crossed my mind, never been a concept. In fact, the idea of marrying anyone had barely crossed my mind, I was just seventeen. Maybe I could have would have liked to have gotten a date with Chuck, for instance, but a ballplayer? C'mon.

"I'm sorry, kid, I didn't mean nothing by it." "There go my chances," was written all over Chuck's face.

"Never mind, I'm sorry, I just don't know what to say," I said.

"Well, maybe I'll see you at another game." Chuck turned to head down the aisle.

"Thanks a lot for helping me, really, I learned a lot," I called after him.

⚾ ⚾ ⚾

CONSTITUTION BLUE BELLES STREAMED INTO the locker room. A palpable buzz filled the room as we changed from our uniforms into street clothes. I bopped over to Kelly.

"10-4, what a great game! How was your night, Kelly?" I began to change as we caught up.

"I met this really cute guy. He said he'd call me. I told him I was 21 so he wouldn't worry about taking me to a bar. I hope I can score my sister's fake ID before he calls."

I raised my eyebrows at Kelly's fake ID plan, then told my story.

"I got lucky myself. I had this really nice season ticket holder helping me figure out where to seat people and explaining the intricacies of the game."

Kelly nodded toward the other side of the room and lowered her voice.

"I bet some of these girls can better explain the intricacies of the game."

I looked over and saw Jacqui, who was clad in matching purple bra, bikini panties and spike heels. I gulped and pulled my baggy Wranglers over my white Sears cottons but couldn't pull my eyes away from Jacqui. I reconsidered the expression *ballpark figure* as I got my first glimpse of a different kind of post-game show.

"If I could just get my hands on that guy's buns, m-m!" Jacqui clucked.

Debbie's head popped out the top of her black slip.

"Wait a minute, didn't he ask you for MY number?"

"You know he did that just so he could talk to ME!"

"No, I don't know that."

"Well, we'll just have to wait and see, won't we? Better get a move on, Deb, we don't have all night!"

Debbie snapped her gum.

"Oh, you know they have to take showers first, and old what's-his-name is bound to call a post-game meeting since we just beat them."

I turned back to Kelly, who now wore Calvin Kleins with a clingy top, her bag on her shoulder.

"No fraternizing?"

"Maybe they didn't hear her," Kelly said.

Or maybe I was a clueless rook.

⚾ ⚾ ⚾

With the exception of the lost date with Chuck, I made out great: $21.25 in tips on top of my game salary of $20.00, whoa. This job would get my college fund going—on top of the scholarship I had won the previous fall.

Like most American girls, I had grown up watching the Miss America Pageant—what could be called the "championship" of Young Womanhood. Every September, Miss America was selected live on television, just before Pop, Dad and the unks tuned in to the World Series, the pageant of American Manhood. Nonetheless, our family's emphasis was on education and good works, never nodding at anything so glamorous as beauty pageants. I went for County Miss, really, for the money, it was a *scholarship* pageant, after all.

Your Great Girl heard during homeroom announcements the previous spring about the County Miss auditions—for seniors with top grades, physical fitness, school involvement and community credentials. I thought it might be a way to help with the serious tuition of Franklin U, Constitution's Laurel League college I hoped to attend.

Though I concentrated on getting the scholarship, my brain got a bit twisted in meeting the challenge of doing something for which I was "qualified" yet unprepared, uninterested even: parading on stage in heels and a swimsuit ran counter to my intellectual/feminist/jock instincts. I had felt personally victorious watching Billie Jean swat fat old Riggs and had in fact been held more rapt by the Women's Lib marches than any pageant on TV. But I wanted the scholarship, so that was the price I paid.

I made the cut and took Poise & Appearance classes that summer with my sister-contestants at The Queen Bee Charm School. Miss Bee, the directress, indeed the Queen, combined a loving motherly demeanor with a withering stare to hold her charges in a straight-backed line. Joe, ever supportive of my derrings-do, tagged it "poison appearance."

When I inquired whether we should paint our nails for an upcoming photo shoot, the assistant Bee, Miss Cheri, snooted: "We paint the *walls*. We *pol-lish* our nails." Polllish. OK, this was getting a little too girly—first I would have to stop biting mine!

But I persisted. I practiced the gown and fitness routines religiously, counting the kick-ball-changes on the living room floor, psychocybernetic-kicking elsewhere. There was money involved. I went for it: I re-re-re-rehearsed, then brought my game to the stage.

I had a great time just being in the show. My family and lots of friends were there. The dashing *Almanack* sportscribe, Tom Dollyson, emceed. He made fun of my name, saying he "didn't know they allowed *guys* in the Cross County Miss Pageant." I proceeded to misquote Albert Camus: "Don't walk behind me, for I may not follow," then channeled a tipsy Billy Joel, slip-noting "She's Always a Woman."

Then, with residual luck, I won. One-thousand dollars and an engraved silver platter. And an old friendship with Tom Dollyson after a while.

⚾ ⚾ ⚾

THEN, THERE I WAS, PARADING at the Lib: in my Blue Belle hotpants and zippered white boots, poised for the National Anthem, the first pitch, the next pitch, the next inning, the next game, the next series, the next homestand, the next season and the next day's coverage of the Blues' Opening Night victory.

⚾ ⚾ ⚾

LOVING BASEBALL BECOMES RELIGIOUS WITH repetition. A baseball fan's feelings, rituals and superstitions about the game rival those of any churchgoer for her chosen faith. Like any deep religious belief, the rapture of baseball is rooted in emotion and tradition. The love for a hometown team is often passed from generation to generation. Think about how you became a fan. Who turned you on to the game? Your dad? Your aunt? I looked again—at my grandfather. Just as spiritual roots are planted, my faith in the Blues started at a young age, before I was even born.

And the more you attend services, the more you understand and honor The Church of Baseball. If your heart and your mind are in the right place, the first pitch is like your first kiss, and you never get over it. You fall in love. It's lovely and horrible at the same time. You can't stop watching after a while. Even when it hurts, you can't look away. Then you know you are in deep. You are in for life.

⚾ ⚾ ⚾

I RODE TO MOST GAMES with Carol Patterson, and walked with her through the Blues office with its bell-logo'd carpet and pinstriped walls which followed the curve of the stadium. I met the Bluesman in street clothes (yes, he was cute in person too) and First Bass Glenn Goodall ("Hiya, Mick," gripping his pipe like Popeye the Sailor Baseball Man) and dapper stadium announcer Duke Braun, and the security chief with the grin of St. Patty, Mr. Dunbar, and just about everyone eventually.

And every night when I got home from the Lib, I would unwind by munching peanuts and Heavenly Hash with my dad, first-hand-accounting the game for him while checking

The Almanack for the previous night's box score and game tale. After really exciting victories, I had to stay up even past Tom Snyder, I would get so keyed up—all that cheering, back to back home runs by Akins and Black, and Moss Thorne unloading his cannon on the opponents' attempting perps.

Chance, MLB Rule 21 &
The Seventh Commandment

I loved my summer job. I worked all the Blues home games. After the second inning most games, things got kind of slow, and the monitoring of fan behavior was minimal. I started getting into the nuances of the game, in particular stolen bases.

Stolen bases will wake you right up, no matter which team you're for, home or away. Perhaps it's the one-on-one competition between the catcher and runner in that moment, personally above their teams' rivalry, which so appeals. The runner teases teases teases, the battery watches for the break, the inadvertent off-balance lean toward second, guilt by association. The homers hold their breath, thinking steal, steal or don't you better not dare.

And if the runner never breaks? It's just another case of at-batus interruptus for the guy holding the lumber at home plate, losing his pitch count if he's not careful. The more I watched, the more I considered stolen bases to be a Venn diagram of interlocking circles. Getting caught stealing can only occur through the coincidence of random chance and near occasion. The runner avoids getting caught stealing—the occasion of sin—by reducing the random chance of its happening. The ultimate reduction of random chance, of course, is staying snugly by the bag, never intending nor attempting to steal at all: if you don't creep near the occasion, precipitate random chance, you can't get caught.

Then, again, if you don't try, you'll never know, and maybe you could've stolen safely, then come in from second on the next batter's hit, and scored the only run in what might've been a 1-0 game. With each play begetting each subsequent play, this is what one guy's steal means, to a game, to his team, and why we spectators love 'em. Double steals even more: can you say André Dawson and Ron LeFlore?

Acting like you are snug by the bag, not even gonna try, may increase your chances of safely stealing, if you make your sole move, evoke chance, at the opportune nanosecond. Yet your near occasion might get tangled in your laces, then stumble back on the bag, just missing the nick of the first baseman's mitt, safe this time, or maybe out.

An event occurs where random chance intersects near occasion, obliging the umpire's call.

Or, here's a change-up: does near occasion occur *inside* random chance, random chance being the possibility of all things happening, avoidance of near occasion then being impossible and certain events therefore bound to occur? With random chance ruling all events, avoiding the near occasion becomes impossible: you might try to avoid the occasion and inadvertently step right into it. The random chance of any given event's happening negates one's ability to truly avoid the near occasion of being declared out rather than safe.

And, sometimes others' interference can influence your near occasion, even as you attempt to stave off random chance.

Then there's positive random chance, what some people call Luck. And that's the argument in favor of near occasion being separate, outside of random chance: by increasing your near occasion, you can put yourself in the position to receive what possible good random chance might randomly happen to happen.

⚾ ⚾ ⚾

KEEPING MY EYE OUT FOR the positive random chance, I had nonetheless applied the avoidance of near occasion rule to good effect with my high school beaux. If there were no near occasion, the random chance of getting caught out was held to zero.

While I avoided random chance, some of my classmates set out to test it during Senior Week down the shore, kept talking about The Playpen this The Playpen that. Get drunk and lose it? I found this trite and superficial: why waste your virginity on some Senior Week fling?

Officially, I was holding out for marriage. Unofficially, I was naïve as hell.

Besides, who had time for Senior Week? My heart had been stolen by the Blues.

⚾ ⚾ ⚾

SOMETIME IN SWEATY JULY, THE game was playing on the in-house cable TV. Kelly and I sat at the Lib's switchboard in our Blue Belle uniforms, spelling the regular operator.

"Mick, you've been holding out forever! C'mon, it's Roe's birthday."

The phone rang, and I picked it up, gesturing for Kelly to hush.

"Hello, Constitution Blues . . . I'm sorry, sir, but I can't see the field from here . . . You're welcome . . . Yes, you have a good night too." I hung up the phone.

"Another call for the score. I guess Carol was serious about the gambling thing. How late into the game do they take bets anyway?"

"Hell if I know, Mick! I'm just glad to have a break from the friggin humidity out there. Oh. Hi."

An obvious gentleman stepped off the elevator and into the reception area.

"Good evening, Ladies. And how are we doing tonight?"

"Great, 7-zip. Tommy's throwing fire, and Jack's hit two—so far," I reported.

The man smiled at me, but as he started to walk past the switchboard, I addressed him in a more official tone, ever the hall monitor. (I mean, just doing my job.)

"Excuse me, can I help you with something?"

He smiled at me and continued moving.

"Thank you, no, just passing through." He whistled away.

Not wanting to be caught slacking on the job, I rose and tried once more.

"I'm sorry, I didn't catch your name, though you look really familiar."

Kelly inhaled.

The gentleman stopped mid-stride in the doorway, and smiled at me again.

"A bright girl with a sense of humor. Where did we get you?"

Still unsure who this guy was, I gave it to him straight, the only way I knew.

"I am—was—Mrs. Patterson's baby sitter, Mary Katharine Carmichael." I extended my right, Kelly silent in the background.

"Lloyd Preston, Miss Carmichael, charmed." Preston

genteely grasped my hand, released, turned and walked
down the hall.

I grimaced.

Kelly cracked up as soon as he was out of earshot.

"Nice going, ace! I'm sure he was charmed. YOU didn't
recognize the Big Mahoff? He's the owner!"

Though Lloyd Preston was an All-Star promoter, his
own photograph was rarely published, and out of respect for
his well-tended privacy, I had never sought one out. (This
was pre-Internet.) I was not going to assume the natty old
guy sauntering through in the squeaky shoes was the famous
Mr. Preston, and I was definitely glad I got to meet him—an
even better reason for stopping him. But I was afraid this all
would sound dumb to Kelly.

I tried to brush off her teasing, but she wouldn't let up.

"Now you have to come out for Roe's birthday tonight
so you can defend yourself when I tell everyone the story!"

Rosemary Duffy was a popular Belle, and they had all
been egging me to come out for weeks. It didn't seem to
matter to them that I was underage.

I looked sweetbread at Kelly and shook my head. Kelly
cheesily smiled back at me and nodded her own, then
grabbed my head and made me nod with her. I rolled my
eyes at her and shrugged.

⚾ ⚾ ⚾

I ENTERED THE BLUE MOON with Kelly and Rosemary.
The dimly lit South Constitution neighborhood
taproom was plastered with team pennants: "BLUES . . .
BABY!", "SKATES: IT'S A SLIPPERY BUSINESS,"
and "WHAT'S ALL THE HOOPLA?" The bartender
filled plastic cups with champagne. We all raised our drinks
for the toast.

"A very Happy Birthday to Roe, may she meet and marry a ballplayer, so we can get her out of our hair!"

"Hear, hear! Go for it, Rosalita!" We sang Happy Birthday.

I was standing off to the side of the hubbub, when Doug Akins caught my eye. He was much better looking than his rookie yearbook picture. The girls were always saying how sometimes the players would show up after games, but it was something else to see them in street clothes. Without the special wardrobe, a priest passes for a regular guy. Next thing I knew, he was approaching me.

"Hey, Sweetheart, have some champagne." He offered me a plastic cup from the line-up on the bar.

A little startled, I said, "No, thanks, I don't really drink."

"C'mon, a little champagne . . . "

He smiled at me, eyes of chocolate kisses, and held my gaze.

I was smitten.

" . . . won't hurt me." I took the cup from his hand and gulped some champagne, then caught my manners.

"Mm. Oh, I'm Mick Carmichael . . . I work for the team."

"Doug Akins." He extended his hand and smiled at me as I transferred my cup to my left hand, dried my right on my Wranglers, and shook his hand.

"Hi." Awkward pause. Another sip.

"Outfield."

Doug nodded.

"Mick Carmichael sounds like a baseball name: Now batting for the Constitution Blues, Mic-k Car-mi-chael!"

I smiled at Doug then stood beside him a few minutes, silently drinking champagne, but I couldn't think of anything to say! I was sure I was blushing. I was certainly feeling warmer. I escaped to the other side of the pub, snuck up behind Roe and planted a big kiss on her cheek.

"Happy Birthday, Roe! Thanks again for the lift over."

"No problem, Mary Kate. Glad to see you out for once! Here, have some champagne." Roe handed me a plastic cup.

"Just one more. Thanks."

I sidled up to Kelly, who took a cup from the bar.

"I wonder why more people aren't drinking the champagne?"

I grabbed another cup.

"So there's more for us, Kel!"

"Take it easy, Mick. This stuff'll go right to your light-weight head, and it'll be over."

"I think it already is . . . "

I ran to the back of the taproom to the Ladies.'

⚾ ⚾ ⚾

I AWAKENED IN A WET bed, head full of fuzz, wondering how I got home, doubting I could make it to the bathroom, let alone the Lib that night. Uhhhh. Puke.

The smell in my mouth tasted like the fumes in the kitchen the time Mom's Mormon friends came for a "family night." All that summer, the two young black-tied men had been stopping by for lemonade. I felt like my mother was sort of leading them on, we were never going to convert, so what for all the chit-chat? Finally, in the face of abject Catholicism, the Mormons proposed a Family Night. We sibs balked at this spiritual intrusion, but nonetheless assembled in the living room at the appointed hour. The Mormons arrived in their crisp shirts and black ties. They had barely said their hellos, and next thing you know, there's a BOOM! from the kitchen. Joe's home distillery above the oven had aged its oranges and peaches just perfectly. The Mormons, well, they went back to Provo, while I helped Joe pick glass shards from the wooden cabinets and tried not to inhale, thanking God for his incredible timing.

⚾ ⚾ ⚾

PRE-GAME, CAROL PATTERSON SAT AT her desk scanning the Belles. "Has anyone seen Mick?"

I heard my name as I straggled in the locker room, certain I must be looking a little green.

"Hi, Carol, sorry I'm late." I smiled weakly.

"That's OK. Mr. Preston would like to see you in his office before you report to your section." Oh, crap.

Carol seemed nonchalant about it, but I could feel my fate darken. I couldn't believe I was going to be fired. I had waited so long, and now after only doing it once, I was in trouble. How did Mr. Preston know I was fraternizing with Doug the night before? He must have spies! And, how would I ever explain this to my Pop? Crap.

I walked the plank past the reception area and down the hall. I had been "called to the office"—to Mr. Preston's office! I thought I had been raised right—even attended Catholic school 'til third grade, when Joe's devilish desk dancing finally overwhelmed Sister X, and we were exiled to public school. Though I never missed the scratchy wool uniform nor the First Friday kneel down-stand up routines, Sunday Mass and CCD lessons had helped me maintain a certain vigilance against the Public Influence—until I buckled under to Kelly, then drank all that underaged champagne!

I was about to be exiled again. I took a bad breath outside Mr. Preston's office and knocked. Suzanne, Mr. Preston's coifed blonde smoker assistant, stashed her emery board in her top drawer as I entered. I put on the cheer and smiled at her.

"Hi, I'm Mary Katharine Carmichael. Mr. Preston asked to see me." I smiled some more: *A spoonful of sugar helps the medicine go down, the medicine go down, the medicine go down.*[†] I thought I'd puke. I knew he was going to fire me.

"Yes, he's expecting you." She stared at me a second, then added, "You're Carol Patterson's *baby* sitter." I misperceived her dig, perking instead at being recognized.

"Well, yes, I was. Haven't actually done much baby sitting since I started here, though." I chuckled at how long ago my baby sitting days suddenly seemed.

Suzanne, disinterested, buzzed Mr. Preston.

"Lloyd, she's here." She turned to me. "Go on out, he's in his box."

Other than in Carol Patterson's opening night speech, I had only ever heard mention of the Owner's Box when spectators would point up from the field seats and wait for something to be thrown from it after a particularly "substandard execution," aka an error. I felt like I should simply paint a red E on my forehead and get it over with, green gills and all. I could always go back to baby sitting. Or maybe not.

Lloyd Preston's binoculars were trained on batting practice. I hesitated in the doorway, then tiptoed down a few steps and stooped to check the angle on the field from this unfamiliar vantage. Preston looked up from his seat at the railing.

"Well, Mary Katharine, how are you?"

I jumped, a kid caught hand in AstroTurfed cookie jar.

"Oh! Hi, um, I'm fine—now that I've gotten over the embarrassment of asking you your name last night. Sorry about that." I smiled nervously at his tie, which had anvils on it, which reminded me of Wile E. Coyote and how much my head hurt.

"No apology necessary, dear. It's nice when I get to introduce myself. I prefer it. What else?"

I could tell Preston was puzzled by my contrite expression. After an awkward moment, I took a deep breath and repented.

"I feel that I've been doing a conscientious job out there, but I guess you can never try too hard. I really like working here, and I hope you'll give me a second chance." *'Tis held that sorrow makes us wise.*[†]

Preston chuckled and patted the seat beside him. I sat.

"A second chance? Mary Katharine, if I were going to let you go, don't you think I'd just have one of my hired hands take care of it?"

"Well, I guess so, Mr. Preston. But it's kind of hard to know what you would do, especially since I just met you."

"What I would do, Miss Carmichael, is hire you immediately to work in my Sales Office."

I was speechless at his offer: a promotion, not a death sentence! He continued to sell me.

"We have a great bunch of girls down there. They're good people, I'm sure you'll like them. And I know they'll be glad for the additional summer help. How soon can you start?"

I was stunned, but I managed to speak.

"Well, I guess I could come in tomorrow. I'll just have to arrange my transportation . . . "

⚾ ⚾ ⚾

LLOYD PRESTON EASED HIS MERCEDES through the blinding bright morning rush on the Freedom Expressway. I listened attentively, enjoying the smooth ride, tickled by my chauffeur's baseball-Pygmalion charm. He had no idea how interested I was.

"There's never been a day I didn't love going to work since I started in baseball when I was around your age. In the Sales Office, I might add. Ticket sales are the backbone of any club. If you don't sell tickets, you can't pay your players, and, boy, are those salaries skyrocketing! The marketing and promotions areas support the sales staff by establishing a team image. From a business standpoint, our farm system could be considered . . . "

"R&D, sir?"

"You are a quick one. I know you're going to work out just great."

⚾ ⚾ ⚾

THE PITTSBURGH PIRATES WERE THE ones who first claimed, "We Are Family." Their kinship concept was furthered by media hype, and the self-perpetuating nature of such a positive attitude lead the Bucs to a World Championship.

When people think of the Constitution Blues, or any pro team for that matter, that's what they think of—the field team. But every Gunninski curveball and Jack Black round-tripper hangs on a tight organization, which, once inside, I experienced as a family.

The Blues staff was a close-knit group of people who worked real hard, then ate lunch and watched soap operas or worked out together and interrupted ticket calls with birthday cakes. One of the staffers would gather singles from everybody and drive over the bridge into Guernsey for state lotto tickets whenever it went above $10M over there. Weekly football pools and the annual old-fashioned spouseless Christmas party rounded out the fun. Their familial culture earned the Constitution Blues a reputation as one of the finest organizations in baseball. Now all they needed was a championship.

On my daily walk from the subway into the office at Liberty Stadium, I enhanced my own championship efforts by genuflecting full faith and obligation at the 12-foot pedestaled bronze of Paul Buchanan, the Blues' legendary owner-manager now up in Baseball Heaven. I heard that Papa Buck had once penciled a woman into his line-up, but it turned out to be yet another press stunt. He pulled her just before game time, saying she'd experienced "unexpected female trouble."

Probably she wanted to be properly paid.

⚾ ⚾ ⚾

I GOT A LOAN FROM Pop for the security deposit on a two bedroom in the Cobblestone section of Constitution, east by the Lenape River, which I would share with my older cousin Carly. Carly is not my real cousin, but what you might call my courtesy cousin—the daughter of my mom's best high school pal, "Aunt" Circe. Between my promotion to the team office job and heading to Franklin U, and Carly's going to art school in the fall, our moms decided the apartment idea was perfect: we girls would save a little money by living together instead of in a dorm, and, more importantly, they would have each other's daughter to look after the other's. They thought.

I was a little apprehensive: I had never been able to keep up with Carly, but I would probably learn a lot. When she was 15 and I was 12, Carly was the one who had explained to me the Game of Love one day after a Little League game. First base was kissing, second base was if you let the boy touch your chest, third was hands in the pants, and, well, I kind of already knew what a home run was: going all the way.

Mom had explained when I was much younger how a man and wife would "fulfill their married love by making a baby." And our laid back health teacher Noreen Moore straightened out the fallopian tubes and the vas deferens. She quoted the flower-power curlicue covered pamphlet, "Growing Up and Getting It (Compliments of Tampax)": "*You shouldn't worry about getting your period at the party. You can carry your stuff with you.*" [†]

I finally got my period at thirteen, just before my parents' seventh witness to their married love arrived. Are You There, God? It's Me, Late Bloomer. All my friends had gotten it much earlier. I started leaking in algebra class and opted for the practicality of tampons after only a single round of the unbearable diaper-like pads. So now I could get pregnant. But that was kind of an aside to my "becoming a woman." I was raised a good Catholic girl—and I bought in—so I was marriage-bound. That was the proper order of things.

It crossed my mind that, mathematically at least, my little sister could have nearly been mine. Though little Chris's arrival busted up the 3+3 Brady Bunch effect, I adored her. It was just embarrassing to know at thirteen that my parents had done It again. They had hit another homer, their Catholicism assuring their defensive indifference in the Game of Love.

⚾ ⚾ ⚾

I TALKED BASEBALL—EVER THE PREVIOUS night's game—with the office guys: silver-spooned Blake Bedford, a dashing descendant of a Constitution forefather; intern Josh Rutledge, an unassuming Laurel League catcher; and computer genius/astronomy freak Hugh Sargent. While we debated, we stuffed envelopes with group outing brochures, the season's near-end pitch: Calling all fan-troops!

"But Tommy definitely should've gotten the win," I said.

"Rules are rules, Mick," said Hugh. "You can't realign the planets."

"But Gunner really did cut 'em so fine last night," said Josh.

"He was good," said Blake, "but Mark really shut them down in the end."

I shook my head at Blake.

"Yeah, but he had no choice, Blake, he put all those guys on base, not Tommy. Ridder's the reason they went ahead of us, so he was only saving his own butt throwing those laser beams in the ninth."

Earlier in the season I had witnessed this Big Bitch Pitch Sitch: a starting pitcher leaves the game with a slim late-inning lead, the relief pitcher loses the lead—only to be granted the win when the last at bats come alive and recover the lead. This seemed unjust on the part of the Official Scorekeeper, for the fella who had thrown the majority of the game's pitches to end up empty-handed while the goat who had nearly wasted his teammate's effort ended up with the decision.

Yet so the whole concept of any pitcher's being awarded the W, when without at least one run having been produced—usually by a non-pitcher—the pitcher couldn't buy a win. A pitcher depends on his teammates' slugging as much as they depend on him for strikes. This tender balance was just another of the many ways in which I was learning baseball was different from other team sports. On a lacrosse team, for example, all the players' actions are similar and performed simultaneously toward one goal, as opposed to baseball players—singles hitters, spit ballers, base stealers, hot corner men—who perform their specialties in sequence and in established patterns. But supposedly good pitching will always beat good hitting.

That's why they're always scouting the next Lefty rather than waiting for him.

⚾ ⚾ ⚾

BLAKE SHRUGGED OFF MY LASER beams, as Doug and his fellow rookie and best bud Bobby Bahnson entered the Sales Office. Bobby was taller and at least as handsome as Doug, with crinkly Paul Newman eyes from days in the bright farm sun and summers playing ball.

The players nodded at the office guys, who nodded back and headed to the computer room, suddenly nothing to say.

"Hey, Cutie." I blushed at Doug's greeting.

Cutie? Whitley Dunning looked up from her mailing list. Whitley was Blake's pedigreed female counterpart who wished but would never be her older sister, the pampered Pamela who had married *more* money. Whitley wouldn't stop staring, and I could sense her straining to hear my conversation with Doug Akins.

"Hi, Doug. Long time no see."

"How've you been?" He said been like bean.

"Great! The day after I met you, Mr. Preston hired me to work inside. Didn't have any celebration champagne, though."

Doug smiled at my self-wisecrack. Over Doug's shoulder I saw Whitley smirking at me. I felt myself starting to melt between Doug's attention and Whitley's stare but composed myself.

"What brings you upstairs?" The players usually kept to the clubhouse.

"Bobby and I are cashing our checks so we'll have some mad money for the road. They only give us fifty a day for expenses." *Only* fifty a day? That was what I cleared!

Bobby offered me his hand.

"How-do. D-A sure wasn't kidding when he told me how sweet you were." Melt. Bobby's big-handed pitcher's grip cradled my hand.

"Nice arm!" I took a breath. "I've really been enjoying watching you guys play."

Bobby nodded and winked at me.

"See you when we get back, Miss Baseball," Doug pointed at me, then turned to go.

Bobby smiled at me.

"See ya, Mick." He knew my name!

I called after them.

"Bring us back a bunch of W's so we can wrap this thing up!"

⚾ ⚾ ⚾

THOUSANDS OF CONSTITUTION BLUES FANS lined up outside the Lib. I checked passes at the dugout fence as fans streamed onto the field for the Anti-Blues Festival, the team's annual fundraiser/fun-day for depression awareness.

Doug eyed me from the home plate corridor. I smiled back, tried to act casual—but, come on, he was a *man*!

Fans got Sharpie autographs on their team yearbooks and posed for pictures with Moss Thorne and Jimmy Simons. I watched Doug return a notepad to a young Blues-capped boy and pat him on the head. I waved over at Kelly, who held Tommy Gunn hostage in the dunking booth. Blake manned the player-fan tug of war: Bobby and Mark Ridley pulled against six preteen boys and a pair of pigtails. Josh Rutledge and Hugh Sargent helped Andres Lopez and Bart Hudson give a hitting clinic. Whitley served hotdogs.

Three hours later, the field was clear, and we Blues staffers sat in and around the home dugout having a recovery beer.

"I think it was successful," said Blake. "The fans always appreciate when the players come out."

"And it makes them think they're human," I said.

"You mean it makes the fans think the players are human or the players think the fans are human?" asks Whitley. I shook my head at her.

"Well, Whitley, we know YOU think the players are SUPER-human . . . " said Kelly.

Whitley stuck her tongue out at Kelly. Kelly stuck hers back at Whitley. How mature.

"The players I've met seem like decent humans," I said. "Tommy's the coolest—and he's so great! And Doug and Bobby are really nice too." I gathered my belongings.

"Sounds like you're primed for *fraternizing*." I frowned at Kelly's ribbing, then turned to Blake.

"Does that rule hold for office staff too?"

"If it's not in the Blue Book, Mick, don't worry about it."

⚾ ⚾ ⚾

THE *BASEBALL BLUE BOOK*, FIRST compiled in 1909, is the pros' Bible, with its prescriptions for salvation. The First Commandment is Major League Rule 21,[†] which is required to be posted in every clubhouse. Rule 21 concerns misconduct, most specifically wagering on games in which one may or may not have a "duty to perform," generally prohibiting any behavior which the Commissioner would deem "not to be in the best interests of Baseball" with a capital B.

Other specified transgressions of Rule 21 include: soliciting or accepting solicitation (read "bribe") to agree to or attempt to lose a game, or (simply) failing to give one's "best efforts" towards the winning of any such baseball game; accepting of "gifts" beyond one's regular due for winning a game; gifts to or violence against umpires; and violence in interleague competition. In the olden days, this would have been lumped under the catch-all Good Sportsmanship. And then came steroids: what isn't explicitly banned is therefore get-away-with-able?

The penalty for most Rule 21 violations is permanent ineligibility, your basic Excommunication from the Church of Baseball. Failure to report a violation of which one is merely aware, though personally uninvolved per se, induces a similar penalty.

I liked to play by the rules—to do the right thing. It was silly hard to see how I could possibly jeopardize the team. I wasn't much of a gambler, nor did I expect to be near any umpires soon; and as a Great Girl I had always given my best effort, so that wasn't a problem. But, what about the "best interests" clause? Might it be in the best interests of the team for me to avoid the near occasion of Doug?

"Just curious . . . " I waved good-bye. "See you guys tomorrow." I turned and walked down the dugout.

⚾ ⚾ ⚾

LOST IN THOUGHT, I DID not hear the clubhouse door creak as I passed by on my way to the elevator.

"Excuse me, Miss, did I overhear you say you were taking the subway home?" Speak of the devil and all those best interests, here he was.

"Oh, hey, Doug." I smiled and it felt stiff. I knew I was blushing, but I tried to stay cool. "Yeah, in some circles I'm known as The Queen of Public Transportation." I laughed.

"Well, tonight I'll be your prince and drive you. What do you say?"

"Sounds OK to me, Doug." I paused and looked down at my feet, then back at him, most sincere.

"I'm just not sure how your *wife* would feel about it." I had finally read up on him in the yearbook. God, you'd think a marriage vow would trump Rule 21!

Doug chuckled.

"My wife? Girl, I gotta talk to you . . . "

I looked doubtfully at him.

"We're split. My lawyer's drawin' up the papers. It's over." Doug smiled sadly at me. I felt like a nosy heel. (But he *was* getting divorced—hm.)

"I didn't mean to get personal . . . " I quick-stopped myself from hoping anything. It's bad karma to disregard someone else's misery, especially when such fall out may seem to benefit you.

Doug shrugged.

"It's only a ride home."

"I noticed your ring earlier, and . . . "

Doug held his forefinger to my lips.

I looked wide-eyed at him, then started to laugh.

"Sure, I'd love a ride home."

⚾ ⚾ ⚾

A HALF-EATEN BAG OF DORITOS and a couple Pepsi cans littered the coffee table. Doug and I lay on the floor. Playing backgammon.

"Well, you two will work things out, you have known each other so long, you can't give up on her now." I made my final move.

"You beat me again! I'll get you yet."

Doug started re-filling the board for another round.

I suppressed a yawn.

"I don't want to kick you out, but I have to report to the park a little earlier than you do tomorrow."

"If you insist."

Doug stood and then took my hand and helped me up—very chivalrous. As we walked to the door, I watched him look around the bachelorette pad. *Cosmo*, *Rolling Stone* and the ARTheater film bill teetered atop the end table next to three dirty wine glasses; a half-toppled stack of old *New York Times*es abutted an arm chair strewn with sweaters and sneakers; balled up socks littered the linty carpet. I was mortified, wondering what he must think. I wished Carly weren't such a slob!

"I can't blame you for being bored with the conversation," Doug said. "I didn't mean to talk about her all night."

"No, no, that's OK. I really enjoyed hanging out with you. Sorry about your troubles." At least he didn't mention the socks.

He nodded.

"Maybe you two can work it out."

He shook his head.

"Thanks for the ear. You're a terrific girl, Mick. You'll make somebody a great wife someday."

I beamed at Doug as I opened the door to the hallway. Our apartment number was painted in black above the doorbell: 302. (I would find out years later that this is psychward code for involuntary committal.)

"Well, whoever he is, he better like baseball!"

Doug leaned forward, kissed my forehead and pushed the D elevator button. He gave my head another quick peck as he got on.

"Night, Mick, sweet dreams."

I called, "Thanks again for the ride!" as the elevator doors closed.

A few minutes later, Carly walked in carrying her gym bag and inhaled deeply, spotting me where I had melted into the loveseat.

"Niiiice aftershave, I could smell it in the elevator. Who was here?"

"Doug Akins."

"You mean THE Doug Akins?" Carly did her one eyebrow lift thing, oh the intrigue!

"Yep." I raised my eyebrows up and down at Carly, withholding.

"I can't imagine you used your feminine wiles to get him here!"

"Ha! Yeah, that's me, Miss Feminine Wiles, Car. No, he simmmply gave me a lift hooooome from the yaaaard." I grinned, the Cheshire Cat who ate the canary.

Carly sat down next to me.

"Well? What's he like?"

"He's, like, technically still married."

Carly scrunched her face: "Drag!"

⚾ ⚾ ⚾

THE BIBLE IS A LOT older than the *Baseball Blue Book*, and keeping God's Ten Commandments, in this case Number VII, was obviously more crucial to everlasting life than Bowie Kuhn's judgment on Rule 21. Nonetheless, the phrase *best interests* kept ringing in my head. Then there was the "Wicked" King James Bible of 1631, wherein Exodus 20:14 had a small typo: the Seventh Commandment stated "Thou *shalt* commit adultery." [†] The printers were fined severely for omitting the NOT, and the Wicked Bible sells at a premium to this day. Apparently one's salvation depends not only on which Book you wield, but also which edition.

Baseball Blue Book or Gideons Bible, I was pretty certain that being a party to the breaking of a marriage vow was bad karma, if you knew what was good for you. We often do— and nearly as often choose to ignore it.

STOLEN BASES, WINTER MEETINGS & TOMORROWLAND

It is a public scandal that gives offense,
and it is no sin to sin in secret.†

O ver the remaining weeks of the season, Doug and I went on some casual "non-dates." He was old-fashioned polite; I excused myself for our involvement: I was really just being friendly, Doug was from ranch country and didn't have any friends in Constitution. But I kept forgetting and failed to maintain my own cover story. I grew increasingly concerned that someone might see us together and get the quote-unquote wrong idea, since he was *technically* married. And I had pretty much fallen for him.

Doug took me to dinner at the Moonship, a popular candle-lit wooden clipper, and we bumped into Carly's old boyfriend. I wasn't too worried what he might think, Jimmy seemed an unlikely informant, possibly didn't even recognize Doug. I forgot whether he was a Blues fan. Besides, who was he going to tell?

Then Jacqui and Debbie, the veteran Belles, spotted me with Doug at the Springsteen concert. I evaded their prying eyes by acting casually dumb, waving and shrugging from two sections away. God, I hoped they wouldn't say anything. Good luck.

⚾ ⚾ ⚾

THE END OF SEASON PARTY was held in the club dining room. All Constitution Blues fulltime staff, coaches and players attended. Despite a fourth-place finish, the tables were set with crystal and china, top shelf all the way, just like the liquor. Mr. Preston raised another cup.

"Here's to our newest fulltimer, Mary Katharine, 'Mick,'" he winked at me, "Carmichael, may she ever have a reserve clause in her contract."

Everyone applauded.

"Welcome to the club, Mick!" said Kelly.

Kel had been tapped as the fulltime receptionist just a week prior to my signing that day. Mr. Preston had convinced me that college could wait a year or two—the team "needed" me, and I could save more money by working before taking on "all that debt."

"No trades here, Mr. Preston!" I answered.

Doug came up from behind and whispered in my ear.

"You better not get traded. I need you on MY team."

I turned and shook Doug's hand.

"Thanks a lot, Doug. Great season. I'm sure we'll be seeing a lot of you next year." Doug smiled at my improvised propriety—knowing he would see me later.

⚾ ⚾ ⚾

OUTSIDE ON THE GROUND LEVEL, I pulled my coat tighter and looked around breathlessly, heels a–click, as I wended my way past the Lib's cement columns to the far side of the park. I walked up to the cherry red Corvette, and the passenger door popped open. I ducked into the car.

"The walk out here always takes forever! But I'm here now." We were still sneaking around.

"You sure are, baby! Give us a kiss."

I kissed Doug, and he revved his engine. I laughed—he was such a boy with his new car-toy—but then I got depressed as he low-geared the 'Vette around the stadium.

"I wish we didn't have to sneak around like this. I want to tell someone, anyone, how much I love you!"

Doug drove out the back gate.

"But, sweetheart, you know it's better. At least 'til my papers come through." We were still awaiting the finalization of his divorce.

"I know. I should be more patient. Things'll be different soon enough."

"That's my girl!"

⚾ ⚾ ⚾

DOUG LEFT FOR FLORIDA TO play winter ball and let me hold onto the Corvette. Feeling top of my game cool, I cruised around Constitution, up Centre and down Hyde, in and out of Cobblestone. But I certainly didn't drive it home to Montgomery. That would have been showing off and, worse, provoked questions I'd rather not be asked.

I drove the 'Vette to work but was sure to hide it on the other side of the Lib, out of everyone's eyeshot. I told myself the extra walking was good for me and tried not to think about how bright the red was.

Driving said cherry mobile home after work one day, I heard a loud, personal honk behind me on South Centre

Street. A 4 x 4 pulled up beside me, and the cute guy . . . it was Bobby!

I waved to him: Hey!

Bobby gave me the nice car wink, then escorted me up Centre and over to the river. Well, I guessed, I could invite him up for a beer. Carly would certainly flip!

I squeezed the 'Vette onto the edge of the lot across from my building, and Bobby pulled beside me.

"I'm starving, you have anything good around here?" There were restaurants all over the neighborhood, but . . .

"Wanna come up for a beer?" It's OK, I thought, I mean, he was Doug's pal, not just another ballplayer.

"No, Mick, I'm really hungry! Let's why don't I take you out for a bite? You take me wherever you want."

"Let's invite my roommate." I said. "I promised Carly I'd eat with her."

"I see, the old two-fer-one, eh?"

Boy, did he have a grin on him. I was pretty sure he was joking.

"Oh, come on, Bobby . . . " He busted out laughing.

"You sure *you're* not from Kansas? I'll wait here." I dashed inside.

"Carly! Bobby Bahnson is downstairs waiting to take us out!"

Carly was ready in record time, approximately 22 seconds.

"Oh, God, do I look all right?"

"He's just another jock, Car. Plus, he's a pal, so relax." Suddenly I was the cool one.

"If you say so, Mick."

Carly and I strolled Bobby down Hyde Street, the whole tour: cheesesteaks at Jake's, a Margarita at Café Copé, rocking Buds to Skidoo Revue at Cobb's Creek. We ambled home on a beer bond.

"You gals are terrific. I should move to this neighborhood."

"That would be fun," said Carly, looking at me. Carly was convinced Bobby was strictly hick. Adorable hick.

"But before I do, ya gotta tell me what the heck these things are." He stomped on a pair of wooden doors slanting up from the sidewalk, jangling the iron latch. The doors appeared on every house, every row, all over ye olde neighborhood.

"Hey, you don't want to disturb your new neighbors, Bobby," said Carly in a stage whisper. "We're not in Kansas anymore!"

"Auntie Em, Auntie Em!" I said. "Those are the doors to the cellar. When these homes were built, the people had goods delivered to the lower level, instead of up through the paah-laaah."

"Oh, and these metal things?" Bobby leap frogged over a black post hard by the curb.

"Why, thoser fer tying up the hearses."

⚾ ⚾ ⚾

DOUG AND I SPOKE DAILY the next couple of weeks, and he invited me to visit him in Florida. I flew to Orlando for the weekend—and reminded myself that though he paid for my flight I didn't have to do anything I didn't want to.

He greeted me at the terminal with a big hug and kiss: to the hotel . . .

⚾ ⚾ ⚾

DOUG CARRIED MY BAG, AND I followed him into his suite. The carpet was bouncy. I took off my shoes and sank my toes into the carpet. I could see the sky and ocean through the sliding glass doors on the far side of the living room. The television was tuned to the World Series: the Boomtown Dockers versus the Cowburgh Stompers—the perennial champs against the brash brat upstarts.

"My dad will be sleepin' in the second room, so I'll just put your bag in here." His dad! I was mortified—his *dad* was staying with his married son and his "girlfriend?"—me!

I watched Doug walk into his room with my bag and sat down to watch the game. I tried not to let the dad news bother me.

Doorbell! I hopped up and ducked behind the bedroom door, leaving it slightly ajar. Doug chuckled as he passed me and opened the hall door.

"Room service!" The bell boy pushed his cart into the suite.

I could hear Doug settle up. I turned and looked into the room: two double beds. I smiled at myself, my unwarranted fear of the unknown. There was always the other bed.

That evening, we met Doug's dad at TGIFridays. He awaited us at a table.

"Dad, this is Mary Katharine. Mick, this is my father." Mr. Akins stood, and I shook his weathered hand. He and Doug shook hands.

"Nice to meet you, Mr. Akins. Doug has told me so much about you." (Not really, but that's what you say, right?)

"Well, Mary Katharine, likewise, I'm sure. A pleasure." Mr. Akins pulled out my chair. "I hear you're a big baseball fan." I sat down, and he pushed me in.

"I love the game, but *fan*'s a little strong for me. I mean, some of them are complete nuts!"

Doug watched me talk to his father. I caught him smiling at me.

"Well, YOU know how some of them can be about autographs and stuff!"

Doug laughed and nodded. I turned back to Mr. Akins.

"Doug's really great about that."

"Yes, I'd like to think I raised him right. He's real polite."

"In fact," Doug said, rising, "if you two'll excuse me . . . " Doug left the table.

I awkwardly filled the dead air with my technically still married boyfriend's father.

"It's nice to finally meet you, Mr. Akins. Doug really admires you."

Mr. Akins nodded at me.

"I'm not sure what you think about all this, I mean his flying me down here to Florida and everything . . . " Did I need to spell it out?

"You're a beautiful girl, Mary Katharine. I think it's great."

I was flattered. I could feel my face brighten.

"Doug's had some problems lately, and though I would never presume to speak for him, I know he really cares for you."

"I care for him too."

"Another thing you should know about Doug is that he doesn't mess around."

I smiled: of course not. But then, what would you call what Doug and I were doing?

"You should see the women that flock around these guys."

I frowned: I had seen them, often in matching bra and panties.

Mr. Akins tried to reassure me.

". . . but Doug was never seduced by that, I never saw him take any of them out."

I was grateful Mr. Akins didn't consider me one of "them." I was still making up my mind.

Doug returned to the table. His dad looked at him proudly.

"He's just always loved to play ball."

Doug winked at his dad.

"Still talking baseball are we?"

⚾ ⚾ ⚾

I FLEW BACK UP NORTH and landed in my Sales Office saddle Monday afternoon, typing and whispering into the phone.

"I miss you. My flight was good. No, no one knows. OK. I'll see you tomorrow. Have a safe flight. Bye-bye." I rapped my knuckles twice on my desk.

Whitley approached me curiously.

"Hey, Mick, are you tan? You look tan."

I turned to my pile of ticket orders. "Oh, do I?"

"You finally went to that tanning booth on Hyde Street!"

"Yeah, I didn't think I got that much color, so I wasn't going to mention it."

Whitley backed off, satisfied with her own explanation. Whew.

But then I wondered whether not disagreeing with something untrue someone else concocted was a "lie" and whether "lying" (white lying) to preserve one's privacy was really lying. No matter about the lying, though: I was fairly certain about the near occasion of adultery.

Adultery. The first time I heard the word as a kid, I thought it was what it meant to become an adult: adult*ery*, kind of like hatchery—becoming, well, adult. But then I found out what it really meant, and it sounded so inappropriate. It meant kind of the *opposite* of being an adult. Adultery was clearly irresponsible, and adults are supposed to be responsible. But they *were* getting divorced and I hadn't slept with him–*slept* with him—yet.

⚾ ⚾ ⚾

RIDING THE SUBWAY HOME FROM Liberty Stadium, I was still thinking about "that tanning booth on Hyde Street."

I quietly entered the apartment toting my overnight bag and drifted down the hall. Carly called after me from the living room.

"Your mom called about your sister's birthday party, Mick." Carly would never rush me at the door and ask about Florida, no.

"Um." And I would never just spill since she didn't ask.

"How many birthdays can one family have? Your poor mother, seven kids!"

I walked back out and stood in the doorway.

"Mom makes a big deal out of birthdays 'cause they're the one day that she can play favorites and not feel guilty."

But what would I tell Mom about missing Trish's party? Bobby was having a bunch of us over that night, and Carly was right—there were plenty of family birthdays. Plus, I didn't really want to hear Mom's concern about my hanging out with the players. And I certainly didn't need her asking how my weekend was. Lies of omission counted too.

"Speaking of feeling guilty, how was your *visit*?" Carly did her one eyebrow lift thing.

I was really glad she asked. I needed to run this past someone, and Carly was the obvious candidate. But she just always made me feel kind of dumb, like I should just know some of this stuff. So lately I had been waiting until she asked.

"He's great, Car. And his dad was really nice to me too."

She raised her other eyebrow: And?

"I loved *sleeping* with him."

"Sleeping."

"Yes—just. But Bobby's having a party tomorrow night, and I'm probably going to stay over there with Doug." I paused. "I think I'm going to have to break down."

"You mean . . . let him steal home?" She loved throwing that one at me!

I inhaled and nodded wide-eyed at Carly.

"Lions and tigers and Blues!"

"Oh, my!"

⚾ ⚾ ⚾

"I WANT MY MTV" BLARED from a large screen television in Bobby Bahnson's rented condo. Doug, Bobby and Mark were jamming, air guitars set to 11.

"Ya get your money for nothing . . . " Doug shouted.

" . . . and your chicks for free!" Mark's, their words.

I entered through the sliding doors from the snowy back deck, stomped my feet and shivered into the sparse white living room. I sipped my half-drunk Heineken and surveyed the scene. A few other gals congregated on the white leather couches. I headed through to where Doug, Bobby and Mark were standing in the tableless dining room.

Post-jam, Bobby was showing the guys his new stereo system: "Audio Research D-150, with the SP-10 combo, and, the ultimate, the VPI HW-19 MK-3 turntable." A pitcher's attention to perfection.

They looked up and stopped talking when I walked in—the big leaguers' attention to pretty young things.

"Bobby, this is great, and the food smells delicious! It's sort of like your own winter meeting." That Heineken had me gushing.

"Winter meetings are haunted by old cigar-and-bourbon men, no place for a nice girl like you," Bobby said. I was trying my utmost to be a PYT and grateful someone noticed.

Just the other day in front of the trophy case, Blues scout John Kohner had apprised me of said winter meeting smokiness—then pinched my ass.

"I heard that."

"Let's just call it a white-washed barbecue! Glad you two could make it," Bobby said, then turned to the fellas.

"What do you guys think? Should we tell Mick?"

"Naah, we should keep her guessin' as long as possible," Doug said and looked at me with a sneaky grin.

I glowed at him.

"Tell me what?" I looked at Bobby and Mark.

"She won't say nothin'," Mark said.

Thanks for the vote, Rid, I thought. I basked in this odd attention from the guys. Bobby put his arm around me.

"Mick, it's like this: us young guys are gonna be the heart of the team next year."

Doug jumped in. "And a few minutes ago we decided that we are going to win it ALL next year."

"We're IT, babe," said Mark.

I gave them the duh face and moved from beneath Bobby's arm.

"This is supposed to be some big secret?" I grinned at them: you silly bears. "We had a great year last year, of course we're going to do it." I hoped I didn't sound too much like a fan. I swigged my Heineken.

I turned toward the couches where the other girls chitter-chattered, then back to the guys.

"And, thanks a lot for including me in the team meeting." It didn't come out as kiddingly as I had intended.

I shrugged and sulked over to Doug.

He smiled and patted my shoulder.

"But, Mick, you're not really ON the team."

I backed up and looked at Doug.

"I have my vested interests, you know." I tried to stay cool.

"But, you don't get paid for *play*ing . . . " Bobby thought he was being helpful.

"If you guys win, I get a ring too." And Miss Baseball wanted one worse than a diamond. Worse than that, I wanted acknowledgment from the guys that I counted—that what I did for the team mattered. Getting a ring meant that you mattered.

See, in Baseball, The Ring is The Thing. Yogi Berra has ten. Major League Rule 34, "The Pennant and Mementos," provides that:

"The emblem of the Professional Baseball Championship of the World shall be a pennant, to be presented to the victorious club each year, and an appropriate memento (read: *ring*) shall be awarded to each player, the manager, each coach and the general manager of the victorious club . . . " [†]

So, *technically*, per MLB Rule 34, it wasn't true that I would get a ring if we won it all. But I knew it to be literally true: tradition held that all fulltime Constitution Blues employees would receive that elusive quarry if our team were the victorious club.

BUT MARK IGNORED MY CLAIM to a potential ring and followed up "You're not really ON the team" and "you don't get paid for playing" with " . . . and, you're a GIRL!"

There it was again. When worse came to worse, guys would always play that girl thing as their God-given I'm-A-Guy trump card. As if: enough said, no further arguing whatever the actual point was.

The Subway Queen's third rail threw sparks.

"If this *girl* weren't selling all those season tickets, you guys wouldn't get paid! I work at least as hard as any of you do, and I can't afford M-T-V!" I noticed the sudden death quiet and alarmed looks coming from the living room and lowered my voice.

"*Please* don't tell me I'm not on the team." I was pissed. I took a deep shaky breath. I thought these guys were my friends—at least liked me, but I had been set straight: I was just some girl.

The guys stood in silence, looking at me.

I glanced down at the white carpet and closed my eyes. I walked out between the couches and through the sliding doors onto the snow-covered deck. Shortly, Doug came out to retrieve me. We said a quiet good-bye to Bobby and headed for Doug's condo.

⚾ ⚾ ⚾

DOUG'S PLACE WAS ANOTHER RENTAL, from one of the guys who got traded, Maxie Tyner, who had married one of the Belles and taken her with him. I looked around. The condo was emptier than Bobby's if that's possible, no life. Or, rookie baseball life: plush carpeting, no furniture.

We opened a beer, Michelob.

Doug rubbed my shoulders. We moved down to the rug in front of the fireplace and watched the flames jump. It had been kind of quiet since my outburst, but we tried to make the best of it.

"God, I feel so much better than I did earlier. I'm really sorry, Doug, maybe it's PMS."

It aggravated me that I felt I had to apologize (everything I had said *was* true), let alone that I found myself pleading that accepted wisdom: *and* I'm a girl. Duh! I had just gotten mad at Ridder for dissing my gender difference, and now? Yet it couldn't be PMS: the infernal calculation said, no, dummy, you're two weeks from your next period. Uh.

"Yeah, that was kinda rough. I'm glad you're feeling better now." Doug kissed me on the forehead.

"I've been thinking about this for a while." I took Doug's hand and turned, looked directly at him. "I've decided, it's you."

He didn't exactly get it, I could see, so I lowered my chin and raised my eyebrows at him, playing my bashful version of "sexy."

Doug adored me and got it.

"If you're sure . . . "

"I'm tired of waiting. I mean, what am I waiting for?"

"Marriage, I thought."

"That would be nice, but I'm tired of waiting, and considering the circumstances . . . I really want you."

Doug leaned over and gave me his full mouth, full of intention. I had been waiting a long time for this, so it really mattered, his intention.

His kisses were hard and fast inside pitches. He was still pitching, hoping I would not call time and step out of the batter's box.

The hitter was getting warm with all the heat being thrown, kisses by the fire, and I undid my top button, then his.

His rawhide fingers worked down the row on my blouse. He knew I could get a hit, I just needed the right piece of lumber.

Tongues swirled as we lay on the carpet, bare chest to bare breasts. Flames leaped in the hearth like fans jumping up to get a better view. The pitcher removed his trousers and whispered to the batter, checking my stance.

"Are you ready?" he asked.

I could hear the crowd chanting:

"Let go, Mick, let go!"—CLAP, CLAP—"Let go, Mick, let go!"—CLAP, CLAP—

"I guess so," I said.

The pitcher throws wild to the backstop as he unzips my fly. On the mound, now off the mound.

"Here, hold this."

I took his stiff stick in my hand, curious how it could be so hard and yet so soft at the same time. I rubbed it—for luck?

And, he's back on the mound. Two more balls thrown, and it's a full count. He adjusts my position at the plate, and thrusts a high hard one up in my wheelhouse.

I tried to take him deep, but a rookie, I whiffed, and he was out of gas.

Game over. We lay there a minute.

"I love you," I said.

"I'll get a towel," said Doug. He got up and left me lying there on the rug, staring blankly up at the ceiling.

Tears seeped into my eyes and rolled down my cheeks into my ears. He didn't love me. I had skipped Trish's birthday for this.

⚾ ⚾ ⚾

THE NEXT MORNING, I AWAKENED feeling ill to the bone and decided I would call in sick. Though I was with Doug, I didn't feel much guilt about calling in, because I had never yet missed a day. I would just tell Kel—she could let Blake know for me. I leaned over and pecked Doug.

"Good morning, can I use the phone?"

"Uh, well, good morning, I don't have a phone." He chuckled to himself. I felt suddenly trapped.

"What? How can you have no phone?" Now I was going to be late and couldn't even call in.

"Maxie had it disconnected before he left for KC, and I never . . . " He couldn't believe the look I was giving him.

I replied with my eyes: I just gave it up to you, and I can't even make a phone call?

"Maybe we can borrow the neighbor's phone. I met them once. C'mon, I'll walk you over."

We put on our snow boots and trundled to the next condo, where a grizzle-faced portly man answered the door, eyeglasses askew, bathrobe straining.

"Yeah, Phone Trouble, come in."

I looked at Doug, who baaa-d his way past our host. I followed him through a living room piled with toys, diapers, and five children: one docile, two wailing, and two waling—on each other.

Doug indicated the phone on the breakfast bar.

Mrs. Suburban Nightmare stood on its far side, smoking a cigarette, scrambling eggs.

I sort of waved at her as I picked up the phone and dialed the office.

"Hi, Kel, yeah, it's me." I tried to steady my voice for my presently bestilled audience. "I'm not feeling well this morning. Can you tell Blake? Thanks, pal. I'll be in tomorrow . . . Yeah, I'm OK. Bye, Kel."

I nodded thanks to the other woman, who looked past my shoulder at her elder son, who held up a fist full of his sister's hair.

The mother rushed over, slapped the son's hand, and gathered up the girl, promising her, "It'll be OK, honey, we'll just get you a pixie."

Yeah, I thought, and better don't forget the pixie dust while you're at it.

Doug and I exited. The air which had so chilled me on the way over felt now so fresh and clean I wanted to drink eight glasses of it. The internal rinse.

Doug dropped me home on his way to the Lib for a workout: kiss, kiss, call me. Carly and I headed around the corner to the Continental Diner for a late breakfast.

"So, was it everything you had hoped?"

I expected Carly would want the scoop. Who wouldn't?

"Pretty good." Lie.

Carly gave me her one eyebrow lift thing—with head tilt.

I wrinkled my nose.

"It was O-K."

"Yeah," Carly said, "it's never any good the first time . . . "

I shrugged. "After all that waiting, it was somewhat anti-climactic."

" . . . you really need time to figure out what you're doing before it's any fun."

I used to be Snow White . . . but I drifted.[†]

⚾ ⚾ ⚾

ONCE CARLY HEARD I HAD finally done It with Doug, she immediately dispatched me to her gynecologist, who sized me for a diaphragm. I wasn't interested in the pill. It seemed a little too pre-calculating, like you knew you were going to be having sex regularly or something, which I did not expect to be. Not to mention the whole Church prohibition on birth control, no matter the type. Then there was the fact that that barn door had already been unlatched—and the filly had escaped.

I returned to Dr. Nicholson when my period did not arrive. What if I were pregnant? There was no way! I wasn't gonna—I—couldn't—not—I—Oh, God, not that. Anything, anything but that, I prayed. I was too young! But I am smart enough. Yeah, but how smart could I be? Just look how smart.

Dr. Nicholson was kind about it as she drew my blood. (This was before those handy pink-stripe sticks were invented.)

"The chances of someone getting pregnant the first time are," the doc shook her head. "Well, I'm not a gambler, but if I were a betting woman, I'd bet against it."

I tried to place my confidence in the doctor, but I wasn't so sure. It would be a little too perfectly bad if else. I held my breath for the answer.

⚾ ⚾ ⚾

I WAS REALLY HURT THAT Doug had not called me since the Event, but I screwed up the courage to call and tell him that I had missed my period, I figured he should know.

"Don't worry about it, you'll get it." Doug was so matter-of-fact about it, it sounded like he could care less about me or the situation. I decided not to mention I had already had my blood drawn.

I attempted to put the potentially stunning disgrace aside until I knew for sure. If it were true, the test positive, there would be plenty of time for feeling ashamed, mortified, cheap, wounded, used and stupid. And Dr. Nicholson had said anxiety could forestall a period's arrival, so I tried to stay calm.

⚾ ⚾ ⚾

BUT I COULDN'T STAND IT anymore, this waiting on the pregnancy test, knowing Doug wasn't going to be there for me anyway. What else could I reasonably expect?

I called him at the Abbott Hotel (Maxie got released and sold his condo) and told him I got my period—why bother him?

" . . . finally . . . Yeah, I'm glad we don't have to worry about that, I mean you have so much on your plate with the divorce and everything . . . Call me, OK? . . . Bye." He was barely interested, as though *he* hadn't been awaiting it. Which I still was.

I replaced the receiver, looked down at the floor, and turned toward my room. Now it was up to me. The phone rang, and I stopped dead in my tracks.

Is he calling back? The phone rang again. I turned, taking a deep breath, and picked up the receiver.

"Hell-o? . . . Yes—oh, Doctor Nicholson . . . Oh . . . "

My muscles stiffened to marble, a blanching façade, and the fog rolled in. I hung up and an ice pick of ice, a deep shocking chill, sliced my spine. I stood staring at nothingness, petrified next to the phone, its bad ring echoing off the walls of my skull. I grabbed my head. I put my hands on my belly. Oh God oh God oh God. Minutes went by, hours, years.

In the faraway distance, I heard Carly's keys in the door, their familiar jingle.

"Yo, Mick."

My eyes refocused at the sound of her voice. Carly looked into my dazed face.

"How goes, Mick?"

I shook my head and forced a smile. I knew if I spilled, Carly would have told me I should have known better than to screw a ballplayer. I didn't need that just then.

"Oh. Better. I got it."

"Well, that's good."

"Yeah." I stumbled down the hall to my room.

Fucking liar! Now you're lying to your cousin, someone who could help you, not some annoying office girl! Now what?

I threw myself down on my bed and silently screamed into my pillow. Now what, now what?!

I already knew what, knew even before Dr. Nicholson called. And I knew what else: I felt like I was going to die. Was dead.

I was hollow inside, my heart might never properly restart. But the voices in my head might never stop! I had had racing thoughts before, but this was a soap box derby marathon straight downhill on the Highway to Hell. Very steep, no brakes.

> *If you lived in London in the 1700s, you could buy*
> *insurance against going to hell.*[†]

⚾ ⚾ ⚾

How dumb could I have been? I understood about the "plumbing," Mom's reference to the inner workings of the gender-based reproductive systems. And I *knew* it wasn't PMS—even as I had suggested it to Doug right then and there. And I was versed in the various methods of protection. But that Catholic-born defensive indifference struck again. Stupid, stupid, stupid! Miss Stupid Ass Cross County, Miss Straight A's. Pretty fucking smart, huh?

What a slut! I knew he didn't really love me, and I gave it up to him anyway, moth to the flame! Might as well lose it to a big leaguer and all that shit. Well, welcome to the bigs. I deserved this, it was my own stupid fault. He was married, for crying out loud. For all I knew, he was not even getting a divorce!

And his dad had been so charming, disarming: "Doug doesn't mess around . . . " No? Well, he was certainly not going to marry me! There was no way we could get married—his already being married was kind of limiting there—duh! Besides, I didn't love Doug any more than he "loved" me, so I couldn't marry him anyway. So, this was all just messing around. Just a big mess around.

I had been off in Adventureland, a fool for a big league fantasy. And now I was the one who was going to have to bat clean up. But not before letting him know, just in case.

And, of course, the big ass kicker: sex does NOT equal love. You really were in Fantasyland, girl!

Look out, here comes Tomorrowland. Scandal Land.

⚾ ⚾ ⚾

Thought must be divided against itself before it can come to any knowledge of itself.[†]

My mind was a tornado of possibilities, weighing the present moment, hardly realizing how a choice made then would have long-lasting effects, even now.

The Virgin Mary was a better man than me, Gunga Din. It hit me: Mary was the first Unwed Mother. But somehow she had remained a virgin. I had not. And now, I just couldn't do it—bear the false sympathy of strangers and stares of neighbors, the certain team scandal. This was a Blues family matter, which would have to be handled privately. An inside, brush-it-to-the-way-back pitch. Like it n e v e r h a p p e n e d.

I had handled life so well until then! Now it was a bad coaster ride, the rickety Wild Mouse of Life. I wondered whether getting thrown off might not be better, but held on for dear life just the same. My emotions were tempest tossed: I would get a momentary grip on things, only to be thrown blind around another corner of consideration, the idea of a choice. After all my training and good-spirited behavior, I had no one I could really turn to. I decided I had to be strong and go it alone.

I also decided that this was the worst thing that would ever happen to me. I couldn't imagine a holier trifecta:

virgin, still-married *ballplayer*, pregnancy! And, if this was the worst thing that would ever happen to me, nothing else that would ever happen could possibly hurt me worse than this. This was Pollyanna Brightside, reporting from the disaster scene: I felt that if I could make it through the next two weeks, I could easily manage the rest. As if I had a choice. As if.

I would never understand why the Pope doesn't permit Catholics to avoid the near occasion of reproductive accidents. Honestly, which is the bigger sin: preventing fertilization or aborting? But according to the guy who wears the most special embroidered game day uniform of all, thou shalt not use condoms even. And, he should know, he's been infallible since 1870—when the First Vatican Counsel promulgated the dogma of papal infallibility—even though he was born in 1927.

The Pentecostals hold that "The man with an Experience is never at the mercy of the man with a Doctrine; the Experience is so total, it shatters the cognitive packaging." [†] Indeed, I shattered to the point of unthinkingness.

⚾ ⚾ ⚾

SNOW FELL ON A NEAR-ABANDONED Hyde Street. The opening bum, ba-dum-dum, bada bada repeats in my headphones, then: "If you're wondrin' how I knew about your plans ta make me blue . . . " The Big Chill soundtrack Maggie taped for me had some great old tunes.

"Jeremiah was a bullfrog" always reminded me of the fifth-grade spring camping trip when the popular Kitty Carnevale had fearlessly leapt off the mossy boulder into the rushing Managawna Creek and rescued our favorite classmate, the very athletic Josie Jones, who had slipped into the milk chocolate water. I had slipped into Doug's Hershey Kiss eyes that first night. Now, where was my Kitty Carnevale? If only someone would leap in and yank me from this sludge!

But forget about suckering someone else into white-horsing it up and marrying me, saving me the trouble—that would be even more dishonorable than where I was already. Besides, who would play St. Joseph to my unwed Mother Mary? Nelson? Marty O'Toole? No, no, Bobby! Right. Ridder? Guess not, guess so, guess again.

I sleepwalked past Dilly-Deli and Jake's Steaks, with my headphones for earmuffs. "It took me by sur-pri-ise, I must say . . . " Was it really a surprise, though? Really? Suddenly, it all seemed so obvious and trite. Held onto my virginity, and that was what I got? Yep.

There was the option of having the baby without its father. The two Decision Tree branches sprouting from that option lead to a) keep the baby or b) give the baby up for adoption. I knew my mom would consider it undignified, but she would act supportive. I felt so ashamed, just mortified—dying at the idea: how could I bring this home? This utter mistake, this personally degrading miscalculation? But why should anyone have to feel ashamed for making a mistake?

I crossed against the red at Fourth & Hyde. " . . . when I found out ye-ess-ter-day, dontcha kno-ow, I heard it through the grapevine . . . "

But, keeping the baby and dragging it through my joyless Mudville, having him or her looked at funny, born of scandal, nahhh. I could just see the headlines: ROOKIE'S SCREWBALL; or GLOVE MAKES THE GIRL GO 'ROUND; or BLUES GIRL CATCHES POP OUT. No way.

Why should I be publicly shamed on top of suffering Doug's care-less reaction when I really needed a friend? And I had been such a friend to him, listening to him talk about—his wife?! Some friend. Yeah, we were tight.

I looked through the plate glass into the empty Café Copé, walked some more, my thoughts drifting with the snow.

Why did it seem the people most "supportive" of unwed mothers' *bearing* their children were the same ones who would look askance at them after their blessed "love children" were born? *Love child*, that's a great euphemism. In the end there's no difference between a "love" child and a "drunken, what-the-hell-was-I-thinking" child—is there, to these ladies?

What would Mrs. Grundy or Silence Dogood say? After being a "good girl" for so long—holding tight to that Sex Equals Love thing, I refused to be anyone's gossip fodder. My mom didn't deserve that, people talking about it. They would blame her for my mistake, but it wasn't her fault at all; she had taught me right, I just blew it.

And I would *not* be accused of player entrapment! The only thing worse than being ID'd as a fan was, God forbid, being labeled a groupie. I was a teammate, OK?!

Frankly, I had only just begun living my own life. I really wasn't ready, didn't want to be, was perfectly capable of being—a mother?

" . . . and I'm just about ta loo-ooze my mind, honey, honey . . . " I felt I was losing my mind with all these angles on the situation, none of the caroms playable.

This was not what I had waited for, held fast to my virginity only to be stigmatized: unmarried, irresponsible, adulterous mother. If I were a child, I wouldn't want some-one "like that" for a mother, I thought.

But giving a baby up for adoption after carrying it for nine months felt an impossible emotional chore, by then the bond . . . I loved babies, but I was so angry at the situation—this wasn't the way my story was supposed to go! I knew if I went through with the pregnancy, carrying the child of a man who stole home then called *me* out, everyone would rally around me and act cheerful and chipper, and that would be as fake as all that Love Equals Sex bullshit. No baby could possibly gestate properly under such false-hearty conditions, were it then adopted out or not.

I stopped outside ARTheater to look at the posters for the double bill: Talking Heads' "Stop Making Sense" and "The Gods Must Be Crazy." Yep.

I continued toward Third Street. I felt the snow crunch under my feet. It was good to feel something, anything in my utter blankness.

And, if this was the Devil's way of letting me know how imperfect I was, well. I never thought I was perfect, even when I won the Cross County Miss Pageant. In fact, that was just a shock, I had been certain that Misty Krossen would win, especially with that name, just perfect, a pageant winner's name. Not just another Irish girl.

God, you are dumb! How could you have let this happen?!

⚾ ⚾ ⚾

I took this stroll nightly, repeating the arguments—playing both D.A. and public defender. Sometimes I would stop at Cobb's Creek, the rock pub, corner of Third.

Cobb's painter-bartender Butch Galloway became my pal over Pepsis and Blues talk. He was a real hometown Constitution boy.

I didn't tell Butch right off I worked for the team. I was actually trying to forget. The Pepsi didn't help, but I would have plenty of time to Budweiser-bulldoze my sorrows after I spoke to Doug.

ZEN MISTRESS, PAYBACKS & YOU MAKE THE CALL

I had debated whether to continue my winter workouts, but opted for auto-pilot, sticking to my routine—both for stability's sake and so as not to attract any undue attention. You know that's always the first thing the arresting authorities ask: "Was there a change in routine?" I went into hiding in plain sight, while counting on running into Doug in the weight room. I needed to tell him before the team left for Spring Training the next day.

A cluster of players and staff stretched to warm down after Noon floor reps with Sugg, the Falstaffian strength and flexibility coach. What I loved most about Sugg was that he didn't treat me or the other females like "girls." He kicked our feet out from under us during the flexsets, just like he did the big boys.' Sugg's equal opportunity coaching bested the benefits of Title IX, insofar as he set an example for the guys: show respect for women as athletes, thereby as people.

"OK, all you Zen masters," Sugg said, then smiled at me, "AND the Zen mistress—back tomorrow for more abuse!"

I grimaced at Sugg's direct hit and rose from the carpet. I wobbled, a bit dizzy, then wove my way through the group still on the floor. I really needed a dose of the Mood Room. I made my way to the corner of the weight room to the nook the ath-A-leets took to for mental relaxation.

"Did you see that new ballgirl? What a fox!" said Mark.

"Hey, Mick, why didn't they give YOU that job?" Bobby grunted. He did another deep dip from his perch: his feet rested on a lifting bench, and his two hands *on fingertips* on overturned steel buckets. (Mine eyes have seen the glory.)

I eked out a smile for him, truly grateful for his compliment, but shook my head.

"I turned it down." As I opened the Mood Room door, I heard Doug's voice.

"She was afraid it would hurt her professional reputation."

Not as badly as giving the wrong guy the steal sign! That really hurt me. I was already struggling with his not phoning me since I told him I'd gotten my period. It's not like we hadn't spent a lot of time together before we did It. I had thought we would continue to see each other. Maybe I shouldn't have lied, but I thought it was the best thing at that exact moment. And now, he's not even calling me—and he's talking about my reputation!

I pulled the door and shut myself tightly into the light- and sound-proof Mood Room. I settled into the comfy leather lounge chair, then clicked three times: a spotlight shined on a painting of the ocean hitting a jetty; the sounds of the ocean swelled; and the chair whirred softly as it massaged my back. The voice-over began:

"Listen to the peaceful ocean . . . Empty your mind of all negative thoughts . . . "

I closed my eyes. The tears welled. It was hard to avoid negative thoughts. The guy on whom I had bestowed my virginity had just made a joke about my reputation. In a major league clubhouse.

"You are one with the Universe . . . " I dozed, and the voice-over continued:

"Once again, Folks, the Official Scorekeeper has given Mick an E for daring to mix with the boys! Last time was the summer after she won the Gym Award—jumped off the roof to prove to Marty O'Toole that it wasn't just a crush, rode in the ambulance with his mom, and suffered the salty wound insult of the Township Police officer, who asked whether she had been "taking anything?"

Taking anything? Yeah, a three-month break from life, no Indian Summer seashoring, no field hockey! Maggie and Angela were real sports being "The Spirit of 76" for Halloween with me collecting candy on crutches, but I was devastated. I would never beat the boys in foot races again.

My body started as one's does when you realize you've nodded off and have someplace you're supposed to be. I turned off the chair, the tape, the light, and opened the chamber, back to the outside world.

"Hey, Zen Mistress!"

Oh, God, it was Sugg.

"How's the moooood?" He drew it out like that: MOOOOOD.

"Hey, Suggy." I gave him a weak smile, hoped the work-out color was still there.

"What's a matter, darlin'?"

"Aaa, I'm OK, just a girl thing, you know?" The biggest blow off line if ever I said one: "a girl thing"—YUCK!—like, "maybe it's PMS." Why did I always default to that cop-out? I loathed myself for saying so, but in this case my hormones actually *were* raging.

"OK . . . If you say so, Zen girl."

I looked at Sugg and almost spoke, then didn't. I knew that Sugg knew I wasn't right, and he could see I knew he knew. But neither of us said anything else. He was such a Zen Master, I imagined he knew it all anyway. He could read it word for word in my face. And had likely seen it all before. Off to the showers.

⚾ ⚾ ⚾

LATER THAT AFTERNOON, I WAS back on the phone in the Sales Office, pitching the season ticket plans, acting badly, like everything was completely normal, like my sour-puss hadn't recently eaten a bad canary. Yes, the one in the coalmine.

" . . . And we have real depth with those young guys who came up the end of last year. You should see Bobby Bahnson working out, he's going to be even better next season . . . Doug Akins? . . . "

This was a tough sell, but I handled it—like a man? Strictly business, tone rock steady, ripping up inside, progestin and prostaglandin soaring.

" . . . Oh, yeah, Doug's a great hitter, isn't he? . . . Two for Plan B? Welcome to the Blues family! I'll send your confirmation out this afternoon. Bye-bye, Mr. Fitz." I hung up and stared at my computer screen. The Space Invaders screensaver took me away.

⚾ ⚾ ⚾

I LAY ACROSS MY BED weeping weeping. My tears had tears . . . te*ars from the depth of some divine despair.* [†]

I couldn't look anywhere without being reminded: the Blues festooned my room. The banners, team photos and autographed baseballs had nothing to say about this, those false idols before me no salve. Though I tried to keep quiet, sobs punctuated my tears. I heard the phone.

"Mick!" Carly called from the kitchen. "It's your mom!"

I wiped the salt from my face and went to the kitchen. I took a deep breath and picked up the phone, keeping my back to Carly—the better to feign chipper for my mom.

"Hi, Mom. Yeah, everything's fine." I turned back to Carly. " . . . Pop? Oh, geez . . . Yes . . . I'll try, Ma. Love ya, Ma." I hung up and returned to my room, plenty of tears to share for Pop in the hospital. I thought that it might be better for him to die than to witness my disgrace—his family's downfall. Then cried louder.

⚾ ⚾ ⚾

IN THE TEAM DINING ROOM the next day, I sat alone eating lunch, half-watching the soap opera which held the other women rapt. I was caught up in my own drama, knowing I had little time to catch Doug before he was gone for six weeks. By then it would be too late.

I saw Doug walk in and toward the kitchen. Bobby and Whitley were right behind him. Bobby spotted me. He stopped in the kitchen doorway.

"Hi, Mick." I put on my most sincerest forced smile and waved to him.

"You guys workout today?" I had felt too ill to hit the clubhouse carpet, especially after the previous day's exchange with Suggy—not to mention Doug's public consideration of my reputation. I had never had a notion of what it even meant to *have* a reputation until I met Debbie and Jacqui on Opening Night. And now I had one?—

and he had talked about it, like it was any of his business. Yet, it was all his business!

"It was a light one since we're leaving this afternoon."

"No trashcans?" (I'm telling you, you had to see that act to believe it.)

"No trashcans." He smiled at me. I felt really shitty, but it was hard not to smile back when Bobby smiled at you.

"Well, Happy Spring Training, Happy New Year . . . What time you heading out?" Just another casual question.

"Soon as we eat, I guess." That's what I figured. Bobby shot me his chin lift and walked into the kitchen.

I picked up my turkey sandwich and idly returned to the soap opera, as the starlet lambasted the stud.

"But I thought you loved me!" Uh—yeah.

I took my paper plate to the trash can, tossed my half-eaten sandwich, and walked through the dining room to where Doug sat with Whitley.

"Can I talk to you a minute?"

Doug considered me.

"Sure, what is it?"

Whitley looked on with interest. I imitated her look, then turned back to Doug.

"I need to speak with you—*privately*."

"I just got my lunch, Mick, can't it wait?" Wait, he said. That's what I had said too. Til I caved.

"Go ahead, eat your lunch . . . but it's kind of important."

Whitley's eyes waxed into full moon. I iced the moon with a glare. Doug cleared his throat.

"Well, it better be short, I'm leaving right after lunch."

"I know. Ten minutes, 200 level behind the plate?"

He nodded.

I started to walk out then turned back and saw Whitley raise her eyebrows in a gossipy grin. Doug shook his head at her. She straightened up.

⚾ ⚾ ⚾

DOUG MET ME IN THE empty bleachers behind home plate.

"I never got my period—turns out I'm pregnant." No preamble.

"Why did you lie to me?" He demanded an answer as if telling him the truth would have changed things.

"At first I didn't want to bother you with it—like I said . . . with your di—"

Doug waved his hand, prompting me.

"Yeah . . . ?"

"But . . . "

"But WHAT?"

" . . . then I thought I'd better tell you . . . in case . . . "

I looked at Doug expectantly. Doug shook his head.

"You're going to have to take care of it." Cold. Just like that.

"'Take care of it?'" My heart was in my ears, now skidding, slamming the sides of my empty skull.

"It's no problem . . . "

NO PROBLEM?

"I'll pay you back when we come home."

He could never repay me for this. I put my hand over my mouth to keep my heart from escaping and closed my eyes: slam, slam, slam. Tears rolled, Doug stood.

"I gotta go." Doug walked up the stairs and through the tunnel toward the office. That's it?

I wiped my eyes, hoping I hadn't smeared my mascara, at least that might be intact. I scanned the outfield, then my focus came back to the foul ball safety net separating me from the field. That's why they have that net—it's like a protective force field. Keeps the regular people safe from the players' hijinks.

⚾ ⚾ ⚾

THERE WAS A LEGACY OF fatherlessness: my Gram and her little brother had scamped around South Constitution behind their widowed mother, staying a few weeks at a time with whatever friend or relative would have them. They weren't unwanted per se, but the effect of not having a father was deeply felt.

⚾ ⚾ ⚾

THE LIB'S DIGITAL SCOREBOARD CLICKED 1:00. I had to get back inside. I rose too quickly, and fell back into the flippy seat. I steadied myself, holding onto the end armrest for balance, then exited the row and walked slowly up the aisle and through the tunnel.

I entered the Sales Office. Bobby stood with his traveling duffel in front of the trophy case, revering the team's history in hardware. He jumped when he saw me.

"I wanted to say good-bye before we left."

Bobby's sweetness warmed me, despite my sadness. But then I wondered what he knew. He couldn't know *that* already, I had just told Doug. I smiled shyly.

"Thanks, Bobby. Good luck down there." I tried not to cry.

Bobby looked me in the eye, steadfast.

"Don't worry, Mick, everything's going to work out."

We stood awkwardly, then both looked up to see Doug walk past the doorway, staring straight ahead.

I bit my lip and looked at Bobby, then at my reflection in the trophy case mirror. Where was that girl I used to know? I lowered my eyes. The blue bell logos on the carpet began to swirl. Bobby grabbed my hand, and I looked up at him.

"Time heals all wounds, Mick."

I stifled my tears, nodding: he knew.

"Bye, Bobby." I ran to the bathroom.

The bathroom was a very clean gas station-type: a single toilet and sink with a mirror above. The flushing toilet and running water barely drown out my slurping and gasping. I spit into the sink, grabbed a paper towel and wiped my mouth. Panting, I leaned stiff-armed on the basin and looked at myself in the mirror. I massaged my sore breasts. I teared up again, then stopped. My eyes were swollen and red. I dabbed them with tissue, tossed the tissue into the toilet, and inhaled deeply, turning back to the mirror. I finger-combed my hair and breathed again. I put on my game face, blessed myself, and exited the bathroom.

⚾ ⚾ ⚾

I KNEW BEFORE I EVEN met Dr. Nicholson, practically in that defensively indifferent moment—certainly as soon as I missed my period—what my fate was. And what I would have to do. It was pitiful—what I had done, what I had failed to do, and what I next had to do. It was almost as if there were no choice, I had no choice, for a lot of reasons. I went over it all in my mind a thousand times, and never came to a different conclusion. Even before I talked to Doug. But now I really knew the next part of the story, and now I would have to act.

I could never have imagined at the time what would come next, after the choice.

If I were to carry a baby and give it up? Well, I had lived in an orphanage. I was cast in the role of a stoic four-year-old, playing the hero who reassured my younger sisters our parents would be coming back from Uncle Pat's audience with the Pope. But my torn little heart knew the rest of the kids' parents were never coming back. They were dead. I also sensed a certain hypocrisy in the caretaker nuns. It was clear to me that they made an especial effort of kindness with us Carmichael girls; whereas their rage reminded those poor orphan kids, daily, that they were damned and unloved. They were very angry kids and misbehaved accordingly. Some of the boys were scary bad. Joe had to stay in the boys' dorm without us. I was convinced something had gone terribly wrong for him at St. Stephen's, he'd seemed so angry ever after. We skirted the recollection only once, years later, when he simply said, "Yeah, that sucked."

Bottom line was, I felt the nuns should have been just as kind to all the children. I hadn't known about Pop's "kindness" to the orphanage—some small silver in exchange for turning his grandkids into orphans!

So, I knew first hand that children needed love to thrive. I had felt the lack of love for the orphans, and I knew I was loved, I was a thriver! How could a thriver consider denying her own child's chance to thrive? Because this kid would not, no matter how,—I couldn't find the love!—get the love it needed. I was unwilling to gamble that another child would end up an angry orphan, feeling unloved, not thriving: an anti-love child.

The Japanese believe that it is a sin to leave a child behind to be cared for by others, hence their face-saving custom— a woman's hari-kari—called *oyako-shinju.*[†] A mother commits suicide but kills her child first. They also traditionally honor the memory of aborted children—the *mizuko*, or "water children." They pray to Jizo, the heavenly monk-protector of deceased children and fetuses, who receives parents' apologies and ritual offerings for having caused them pain. There are not many adoptions in Japan.

I considered the idea of karma and the circumstances under which this mess began, and found it difficult not to blame myself: what goes around clearly comes around. An abortion would save a lot of people a lot of trouble, but I doubted it would improve the karma. It was awful to even think about.

Forget arguing *in favor of* an abortion. How could anyone ever think of abortion as a gung-ho thing? And what business of anyone's is *my* conscience? *For why should my freedom be determined by someone else's conscience?* [†]

The Decision Tree kept leading me back to something which I had never considered—never dreamed of being in a position to *have to* consider. And yet it seemed somehow the responsible thing to do, to minimize all the potential drama, to maintain my privacy about my thrashed identity, to keep hidden my mistaken belief in Love and Baseball, to make that choice. Decision scientists tell us that people tend to avoid risk when seeking gains, but choose risk to avoid losses.[†] I decided to risk everything to avoid further damage. Now that I had a reputation.

Being a believer—a Catholic even, as I mulled abortion like never before—I believed I was already forgiven. And I considered that choice, taking that risk, *a leap of faith.* Though my faith was begotten by religion, I believed my faith now had to stand alone, separate from the Catholic Church on this one. No matter what the Church said, I had been taught that Jesus had died for my sins. It was all one big sin. Major leaguer indeed. And I was already forgiven. In God's eyes anyway.

Could I possibly conceive of an abortion as a moral choice? See it as a mercy killing?

I feared I would resent the child for the rest of my life if I had it and kept it. Growing up resented is not healthy for a child. *The Denver Post* won a Pulitzer for a study of missing children: most were either tug-o-warriors involved in custody disputes or runaways. Sounds like loveless resentment and pressured pregnancies. Might those kids not better go missing before even showing up? (*Freakonomics* said so.)

I considered the larger whys and wherefores of abortion beyond my immediate circumstance. There was that oh, you might be killing the next Jonas Salk, or the one who would cure cancer argument. But the mathematical probability of murdering a genius is 1 in 500 *trillion,[†]* which means the odds are just as great or small of aborting the next Voldemort. We perchance take the good and the bad. Statistics aside, what is taken by abortion is a sole chance: the distinct entwirling of the genetic codes carried by that *one* sperm to those contained in that *particular* egg only happens once.

⚾ ⚾ ⚾

BLAISE PASCAL CHOSE TO BELIEVE in God to avoid the consequence of his being wrong were he to choose otherwise. I had to believe I was pre-forgiven in the Cross because I couldn't bear to measure the consequence of being wrong otherwise. There is a certain irony to the Cruxifiction in the face of Thou Shalt Not Kill: Jesus's death on the Cross is the literal crux of Christianity, yet it itself is the Big Kill. (And he had already been alive for 33 years.)

In a way it wasn't even a choice, so much as an algebraic equation with a few big, unsolvable unknowns, to which I assigned risk factors, Degrees of Difficulty—like the scoring for diving. And I was pacing atop a tall cliff, with imaginary bookiemen laying money on my belly-flop.

My painstaking calculation approached the mystical certainty I felt about it from the start, like infinity. But was this Mystical Certainty in capitals, my first truly direct experience of "the ultimate"—God, reality? I felt terror at the loss of boundaries, yet bound in a union with the mystical, the unknowable. Was this the Telling Voice, the murmur of the universe, speaking the truth to me? Perhaps I was hearing my inner voice for the first time. All those other times I had heard voices within, they were just the echoes of other peoples' expectations.

The heart has its reasons
which reason does not know.[†]

The Great Girl couldn't find the love.

I could not live on the pedestal any longer. I had started teetering as soon as I set foot in the Lib and began worshipping at the Church of Baseball. I thought it was love, but now, the love, the love, all the love I had ever felt, was gone. I had to get a little cold to deal with it and cut myself off for a while. Life is about reality, not love, girls, and I had been thrown a yakker. I just prayed it wasn't a twin killing, the surgical steal.

GROUND ZERO, TRUMPED BY THE DEVIL & KNOWINGNESS

I hated having to call on Maggie, but I was glad I could and did; Trish was as weak-kneed with medical procedures as I was, and this was no mere procedure. Mags was tough. She would help me get through.

Then there were the family planning counselor's hands on the clipboard, Bic-clicking my stats, black ink staining my Permanent Record: Age, Education, Race, Religion, Profession . . . Therapeutic Abortion.

My legs in stirrups, the masked man's unforgiving eyes at the bottom of the table.

I heard Doug's voice: "Take care of it."

Maggie and I exited the red brick building of Townsend Suburban Clinic. Getting in was one thing; getting out another. We were swarmed by protesters. We struggled past the now-shrieking women and men who spit rage in our faces. One of the women looked like Mom. She yelled to me.

"You're a winner, kid!" The sarcasm burned my soul. Devil as doppelganger.

Maggie and I rushed to the train and tried to catch our breath.

I stared blankly out the train window. Maggie sat close beside me, holding my hand. My head was its own brand new cable station: The Guilt Channel. The sounds and images screamed down my baselines, a stream of consciousness of foul balls:

Pop's voice: " . . . Atta Girl!"

A mass anti-abortion demonstration in Washington. Women carry protest signs: "Abortion Kills a Living Child," "It Could've Been You."

Sinatra: "It had to be you . . . "

My First Holy Communion, received from Uncle Pat: "The Body of Christ."

A pro-choice rally in MetroCity, women waving hangers and shouting: "Stay out of my bed!"

The crackle of a newscast: "A family planning clinic attack leaves a doctor dead and three patients wounded."

I drew a "#1" on the sweating train window and shivered. I cried a little and my body convulsed. I almost puked. Maggie sat by and held my hand through it all.

The train lurched into West Constitution Station. Maggie hugged me good-bye.

"Call me, Mick, 'K? Anytime." She squeezed my hand. "I love you."

I whispered, "Thanks, Mags." I sank into my seat. Maggie waved back and got off the train. I thought I could make it home alone. I wished on a falling star, at least that's what it looked like through the misty window. I could not tell I was weeping.

⚾ ⚾ ⚾

BY THE TIME I GOT home, it was dark. My eyes were sore from crying. I entered the apartment on quick tiptoe to avoid Carly.

"Mick! Where have you been?! I've been worried sick . . . "

I jumped at Carly's voice and headed straight to the bathroom. I was sure she could hear me vomiting. She was quick at the door.

"Mick! Do you need help?"

"Yes . . . please." I was shaky and moaning like a mother who had lost her child.

Carly slowly opened the door.

I knelt at the toilet. I looked up at her.

She put her hand on my shoulder, waiting for me to speak first.

"I'm really sorry, Car."

Carly shook her head at me: don't be sorry, what is it?

"I just came from the clinic. I called Maggie this morning, she went with me."

"Huh? What are you . . . " She took her hand off my shoulder.

"I'm sorry I lied to you. I never got my period." I started sobbing.

"Why didn't you tell me?! I would've gone with you! I would've done anything for you!"

I wailed. Why hadn't I told her? I couldn't ever tell her that.

A few moments passed. I calmed down a bit, then Carly spoke gently.

"Did you tell Doug?"

"Yeah."

"What'd he say?"

"He just said to 'take care of it.'" I broke down again. The triple play of emotional, mental and physical pain took me to my knees. I feared I could not feel my heart beat because it had frozen in time at the Townsend Clinic.

"Bastard!"

> *It is one of the superstitions of the human mind to have imagined that virginity could be a virtue.*[†]

And to think that I had worried whether I might never get to do It before nuclear war (inevitably) occurred.

I remembered my 8th grade history professor Remy Mabilliard's saying, "When it happens, I hope to be at ground zero."

"What's ground zero?" I had asked.

"The epicenter, you're instantly obliterated, no waiting around for the radiation to eat you alive. Ashes to ashes, Mary Katharine."

At the time it had sounded better than "putting your head between your legs and kissing your ass good-bye," Uncle Frank's account of his grade school daze.

But now that I, the me I knew, had done It and was now dust, I wasn't available to argue against being gone. My own nuclear winter was setting in just as spring was arriving. I was a void, a physical body carrying around a—well, nothing—emptiness. A well of emptiness. I had always been terrified of Gene London's bottomless pit, and now I had fallen into it.

⚾ ⚾ ⚾

TWO WEEKS LATER ON A crisp spring afternoon, I dragged my sorry self out of the pity pit and walked up Spaight Street to St. Anastasia Hospital. A nurse directed me to the Pulmonary Unit. I could hear the sounds of a ballgame from a room down the hall: good, he was still tuned in— even if I wasn't.

I entered the room and sat at Pop's bedside, holding his hand, watching our Mango League game. He mostly dozed, but I knew he was glad I was there.

I went into the small bathroom and checked: still some bleeding. God! If it would just go away. Then I could begin to forget the whole thing.

I re-entered the room. Who was I kidding? I would never be able to forget.

"Seen your mom lately, Katie?" I jumped at Pop's voice.

"Not as much as I'd like to, being so busy with work, you know."

"She misses you, you know."

I nodded.

Pop looked at me and gripped my hand.

"At least the bums are winning a few for you." He wheezed, a consumptive leprechaun rounding his last four-leaf clover.

I forced a smile for him.

⚾ ⚾ ⚾

AT WORK ESPECIALLY, I PUT up what I thought was a brave front, but Kelly wasn't buying, she just didn't know what was wrong. I passed by the switchboard a week before the Opener.

"The guys are really cleaning up down there, huh, Mick?" She tried to engage me.

"Certainly makes it easier to sell tickets. I hope they can carry it through the regular season." Lord knows I couldn't, I thought. The rip I couldn't resist, nor could I mend.

"If they do, I might even watch a game!" Kel was never into it like I was, and her self-kidding was much kinder. I appreciated her attempt, but I just couldn't get into it with her: Kel was my great friend, but she was also the switchboard operator. There would be too much pressure on her not to talk. I didn't want to burden her with a story she could never share.

But, God, I was a mess. A puddle of nothingness.

⚾ ⚾ ⚾

BUT I REFUSED TO GO to confession over it. Tell a priest—some *man*, who's supposed to represent *God*—I need a middle man to talk to God?—that *I* was to blame, responsible: to take the fall, play the goat, admit I'd been suckered by the Devil himself? *The devil made me do it, Geraldine.*[†]

I had made myself sick at seven, heading into First Penance, straining to think of something I had done wrong. Finally I settled on that time I had *considered* Mom's pocket change. Guilted by Sister X into making something up, I effectively lied to a priest: "Father, I *stole* my mom's pocket change."

Now, not only was there a middle man, but one had to make a "good" confession in order to qualify for First Holy Communion. That "good" right there is one of those undefined/undefinable terms, open to interpretation, like "inalienable rights." Who says what constitutes a "good" confession? Who grants those "inalienable" rights?

In a rush of clarity, I apprehended the patent *wrongness* of a second grader's feeling pressured to make something up—essentially TO LIE in order to have something to say to the priest in the confessional. This was obviously not a "good" confession! But I felt it might be over doing it to admit my lie in the confessional moment. ("And, Father, right then, when I said I *stole* my mom's change, I lied to you, I only *considered* stealing it. I had only been trying to please Sister X by lying to you!")

What a sin of mental gymnastics—making little seven year olds trump up charges against themselves in order that they may receive the Sacrament of Absolution! I was extremely confused by this don't ask-do tell practice of lying in order to have something to confess, so had gone along for getting along's sake. Now I got it, and I was furious! What happened to the inalienable right to take the Fifth? As far as I knew, one could not be compelled to speak against oneself. They had me confessing to crimes I hadn't committed. It was impossible to put spiritual stock in that operation any longer. Some children *are* innocent. Like the orphans.

⚾ ⚾ ⚾

I WAS SO DESPERATE FOR a friend, I decided to what the hell tell Butch Galloway the story, he was enough of a stranger, but enough of a pal. I grabbed a cheesesteak at Jake's, then headed to Cobb's Creek for a beer and some Butch.

"Hey, it's Mickey Mouse!" Butch had so dubbed me when we first met and I had explained my nickname.

He pulled me a Bud, 50 cents.

"Butch, I need your professional ear."

"That's why I'm here, Mouse."

He was so sweet. And cute too, in a jaunty kind of way.

"I just," I started to tear up, shook my head and sipped my beer.

"What, Mouse, what, oh, don't cry." He reached over and dabbed my face with a cocktail napkin.

He was so sweet, he almost didn't mind my crying.

"I just, I'm trying to stay calm. I just got kind of caught up in a bad situation, and," I sipped my beer, dropped another tear.

Butch walked down the bar to serve another customer, but he came right back. He was so sweet.

Butch had spotted Mouse's troubles the first time she walked in: she was so stoned she left her headphones on after making jukebox picks, now changed from Pepsi to Bud. So, she was finally gonna spill? Probably a boyfriend, always was.

Butch gave great ear, and he knew how to make a girl feel special. He got me gently drunk, took me home and what-the-helped me break in my diaphragm. Time to lift that curse.

After my friendly, one might say *sporting*, experience with Butch, I was convinced that the guys had it right: Forget the love thing—sowing wild oats was where it was at. Just remember to WRAP YOUR BAT.™

⚾ ⚾ ⚾

WILD OATS, INDEED: I WAS no longer myself. I was not the same person.

When I would speak, I felt like a ventriloquist inserting words into my own mouth, scripted words, the expected words. My life felt like a movie I was watching while I was living it, which out-of-bodiness, while oddly sensational, felt B movie trite as soon as I described it to myself as such: "out of body," "like in a movie." This whole matter was trite.

I was ever in the cover pose, game-facing it, acting for the audience of everybody like I was JUST SUPER. I lip-synched myself, the words of possibility (Go, team!) no longer vested, blindly accepted, now empty backstop-less words: faith, hope and love. And the greatest of these is love? And *making* love? What a terrible joke on me! Sex is JUST FUCKING. Now they tell me.

I would have to play this new role I had slipped into as it unfolded, on my own, making up the rules as I went along, taking each situation on its own merits. Moral relativism is what it's called these days. In 1999, then-Vatican doctrine chief Cardinal Ratzinger, while warning against moral relativism, indicated that "judging a Catholic politician's vote on abortion legislation as sinful must take into account circumstances, freedom, intention and *informed conscience*, and that ultimately the question lies between the person and his or her confessor." [†] All this consideration in judging a politician's *vote* on abortion? What about the circumstances of a freshly-deflowered virgin, what of her "freedom, intention and informed conscience?" Oh, my confessor friends and moral relatives, was I heartily sorry.

This Great Girl's informed conscience concluded that I was both pro-choice & pro-life. Pro-life & pro-choice. To some people, that's like saying you're both a Mets and a Yankees fan—impossible!—you're either one or the other. But *is* it impossible?

Pro-choice & pro-life are not mutually exclusive states of being. In fact, they strongly support and balance each other, defusing the politically-charged pro-life/anti-choice and pro-choice/anti-life dichotomies. If you are pro-life, you should be pro-*everyone's* life, starting with girls' lives by properly educating them as they *grow into* women. If despite *proper* sexuality education one of those young women—who is already alive—becomes pregnant, and in a given moment believes in her heart that she must make a horrible choice but an unavoidable one, we must be pro-choice in supporting her, because *her life already exists.*

As for the fear that sex education promotes sexual behavior, the notion of "good girls" is well-outdated: the best sex ed classes would frankly emphasize practicality over virtue. "Unknowingness" must be removed as a reason anyone ends up in the position of choosing abortion. And we must not play Puritan when it comes to following through on the knowingness once we know. That was my Catholic "good girl" mistake—having the information about birth control yet not using it because it was against Church teaching. This type of thinking calls for an immediate separation of church and state!

Further, our men must call on boys to be "good" too, by taking responsibility for their sexuality and the health-safety of themselves and their ladies: Before you swing, WRAP YOUR BAT™!

Minimizing errors? In the Game of Love that is something both Mets and Yankee fans can agree on.

> *Without doubt, the greatest injury . . . was done by basing morals on myth, for sooner or later myth is recognized for what it is and disappears. Then morality loses the foundation on which it has been built.*[†]

My sexual freedom was countered by a sense of terror of that freedom. Moral relativism becomes a wasteland. I became untethered. The Great Girl drifted.

⚾ ⚾ ⚾

I STUMBLED INTO THE DARK kitchen. The glow from the TV was the only light.

Peter Pace, Constitution's favorite sports reporter son, murmured from the screen.

"Yep, just a few more days, and I take the leap . . . "

The kitchen light snapped on.

I jumped and fell into the counter in my purple polyester teddy.

Carly stood beside the light switch looking disgusted.

"Oh, hi, Car. I didn't realize you were still up."

Carly rolled her eyes at me.

I opened a cabinet and got out a glass, smacking it to the counter.

"Mick, what are you doing?"

"Jus' gettin' a drink a water." I turned on the faucet. Water rushed out.

"No, Mick, you know that's not what I mean!"

I turned the water off. Carly lowered her voice.

"How many *dates* have you had this week? It's like a different guy every night."

I stared at Carly over the rim of my water glass.

"Cut me a break, Carly." I paused, then mumbled, "You're jus' jealous." I raised my eyebrow at her.

"Jealous? Of what, Mick? Being a sleaze? You need professional help! When's the last time you visited your family?"

I started to cry.

"I can't go home, Carly. It's not that easy. Let's drop it, OK?" I nodded toward the hallway. "I don't think now's the best time to get into this." I wiped my eyes. The strap of my teddy slipped.

"There never will be a good time, Mick—and with this AIDS thing they've been talking about, I'd think you'd be smarter than this!"

"I use condoms." I answered coolly. "And, besides, my karma can't really get much worse." Of that, I was convinced.

I jagged to the coffee table and found Carly's roach in the ashtray.

"Can I have a hit?" I was shivering.

Carly walked over and sat beside me, putting her arm around me in my Frederick's of Hollywood knock-off.

"Only if you promise me you'll get help."

I lit the roach and took a big puff.

"Yeah, sure, I'll get help." I got up and headed back to my room with my water glass. "G'night, Car."

Carly settled back down at the TV.

"This is Peter Pace, live from Florida, where the Con Boys won today, 8-5."

Carly called after me.

"They won today, by the way."

"Yeah. We open Tuesday."

The TV voice-over announced, "This rebroadcast of tonight's 11 o'clock news is presented as a courtesy to our late night viewers . . . "

Carly clicked off the TV.

The screen spiraled to black, followed by the crash of glass.

AIRPLANES, HEXES & THE PSYCHIC FRIENDS NETWORK

Red, white and blue bunting hung on the baseline fences. The large scoreboard in centerfield said: "WELCOME TO OPENING DAY." Liberty Stadium filled rapidly with eager fans. It's always such a long time from October until April!

Then, it's Opening Day again: spring, eternal, hopes! Everybody has the same record: no wins, no losses. Well, we had one big one, but it wasn't on the record—just my Permanent Record.

Behind home plate, I corralled a group of children in ruby red choir robes. I noticed over at the fence a perfect-looking blonde in about a size 2 Blues jersey. "LIZ" signed an autograph for a slobbering paunchy fan.

One of the choir boys nudged me.

"Is that the new ballgirl?"

"You got it, slugger!" Just the facts, Ma'am.

"She's pretty!" said a choir girl.

I cringed at the girl's innocent pronouncement, as Duke Braun came on the public address system.

"If you look overhead, Ladies and Gentlemen, you can see Peter Pace's escort, a Piper Cub."

The choir boy pointed up at the sky.

Pace's airplane circled above Liberty Stadium, as Braun continued.

"In a few minutes, he'll deliver the first ball, and our season will begin!"

Fans whistled and yelled from the bleachers.

"Yeah, Pete!" "Go, Blues!"

The PA could just be heard over the crowd's cheering and the Piper's engine.

"OK, Folks, here he comes now! Five, four . . ."

The crowd joined in for the countdown.

". . . Three, two, one . . . !"

Peter Pace waved and leaped from the airplane. His parachute did not open. Did not open!

People shrieked as Pace plummeted to his death, slamming onto the AstroTurf in centerfield.

I pulled the choir kids close, needing them as much as they needed me. Their whimpers echoed in the tunnel behind home plate. I whisked them off the field.

A paramedic unit rushed by us onto the field. All I could think of was blood—how it kept us going and how its loss stopped us in our lively tracks.

In the bleachers, mothers clutched their children, covering their eyes, bowing their heads.

Through their own tears, Blue Belles attempted to comfort the fans.

On the upper level concourse, fans huddled in impromptu groups, some kneeling and blessing themselves. Others, sobbing, stumbled down the exit ramps, fleeing through the gates, hurrying to their cars without looking back.

The remaining crowd watched in silent horror as the

paramedics raced out to centerfield to recover Peter's body.

I took the choir children to the Sales Office to meet their parents, then headed upstairs to see what was next.

In the Owner's Box, Blake and I stood by as Lloyd Preston spoke quietly on his dugout hotline with the umpire crew chief, Eddy Doyle.

"It's a sellout crowd. If they can take it, I believe we should proceed with the game." I looked at Blake and shook my head as Preston hung up the phone and turned to us, smiling stiffly.

"A nice, solid win might take the sting out of it for them." No sale.

Blake nodded at Preston. All they saw was my back as I exited the box.

Back inside the Lib, the PA blared to a near-empty stadium.

"Ladies and Gentlemen, thank you for your patience. Game time will be 2:30. Please join us in a moment of silence in memory of Peter Pace at that time."

⚾ ⚾ ⚾

INSIDE THE SALES OFFICE, POST-GAME stock was taken.

"Team zero, news team zero," I announced.

"God, that's morbid, Mick!" Hugh said.

"It's been a bad day for everybody, Mick," said Whitley, "exspecially Peter."

"At least they could've won after that. Or even tried! What, about five booted balls?" I didn't know if I was more spooked or disappointed.

Blake remained an Opening Day optimist.

"Lighten up, Mick, there are 161 more games to go."

"Yeah, thanks for reminding me."

Hugh, Blake and Whitley exchanged looks: What's up

with Homer Girl?

I said nothing.

⚾ ⚾ ⚾

AT THE REAR OF THE stadium, Doug's red Corvette waited in its usual spot. Doug looked up at the sound of the passenger door latch and beamed.

"Well, I'm glad you decided to come out tonight." He watched Liz adjust her leather miniskirt as she squirmed into the bucket seat.

"I just couldn't go right home after a day like this. That poor man! You were so nice to distract me while they were cleaning him up."

"My pleasure, darlin.' Now whaddya say we grab some beers and head for my place and forget all about it?"

⚾ ⚾ ⚾

PEOPLE WERE LINED UP AROUND the block to get into Neumann Cathedral.

Last time I had been in that neighborhood was when Maggie and I got lost near the Main Library during the Bicentennial Celebration. We met these cute boys watching the parade, and the rest of the family had wandered off down Allegiance Allee without us. The old Italian man with the water ice stand recognized us by our matching Adidas Pop had bought us for lacrosse. (Years later, Dad would catch a purse snatcher nearby, red bobos leaping the library railing, coming to the aid of a damsel Russian tourist.)

I got out of the cab and rushed into the cathedral. I looked up the long aisle and saw the casket draped in gold-embroidered cloth and the burning funeral candle. Then the incense hit me. I felt so dead, it affirmed me.

I got in line for Confession. When it was my turn, I

entered the dark box and knelt down, crossing myself. Maybe this would help.

"Bless me, Father, for I have sinned."

"Yes, my child."

The disembodied voice was muffled by the curliqued wooden screen, but it was Uncle Pat! What were the odds I'd pick his listening booth? But I certainly couldn't get up and run out, so I did the only thing I could, I continued.

"It's been . . . um . . . a-bout . . . uh, nine months since my last Confession . . . "

Though I was sure by then he recognized the voice he heard, Uncle Pat maintained his priestly-professional tone.

"What can I help you with?"

"I . . . I . . . need to be forgiven. I've dishonored God . . . and my family. I had an abortion. I am so very sorry."

"Your sins have already been forgiven through Christ's suffering on the Cross."

"Thank you . . . Father." Nice reminder—I had thought of that too—but: *premeditated murder*?

One of the strongest group traditions, religious or otherwise, is the implied promise not to tell, to keep the quote-unquote trouble shhh quiet, even among and between members of a given family. This willful ignorance of one's young—which is to say keeping certain truths from the kids for the sake of "sparing" them—is often enforced merely for continuity's sake: after telling a couched version of a story for decades, which revision has become the legend, why go and change the tune and "ruin it" for everybody? This secret-keeping holds as true in the Catholic Church family *and* the baseball family as the Omerta does for Joe Bagadonuts and his friends' friends.

I trusted Uncle Pat would never mention it.

He said the blessing and assigned my Penance: ten Our Fathers and ten Hail Marys. But if he knew the whole story,

I thought, he'd have me say ninety novenas—in Latin! But really, enough prayers couldn't possibly be said. Somebody hurl me a Hail Mary Hall Pass.

I exited the confessional and slinked up to the front pew, where my family was assembled in various states of mourning. I touched the casket and slid in next to my dad.

Twenty priests, in pairs, followed Uncle Pat up the cathedral's center aisle. He paused and rested his hand on the casket, then stepped up onto the altar, where he lead the concelebration of Pop's Mass of Christian Burial.

I went to Communion with my family, then sat between Maggie and Trish, weeping in the pew. Little Chris wasn't sure about any of this. Denny's birthday buddy was gone.

The pallbearers rose. Joe, Tom, Nelson and Uncle Frank lifted Pop's casket and walked him down the aisle that one last time. We others followed to the vestibule.

Greeting the mourners took everything I had in me. I felt like such a disgrace to Pop's friends—who ALL wanted to talk about the Blues.

But Uncle Pat said I was already forgiven! Why, then, did I feel so bad?

I was in my head through most of the Irish wake, the death/murder/forgiveness/redemption wheel ever-tightening around my soul, condemning myself, saving everyone else the trouble.

Mom drove me home after the luncheon. It was a quiet sad ride, surprisingly quick in the end. We pulled up to the curb in front of my building. 3-0-2, here I come.

"Thanks for the ride, Ma." I leaned over and hugged her. We were both weepy. "I'm going to miss Pop so much!"

"Me too, honey."

I wiped my tears and grabbed the door handle, tried to smile.

"Well, I love you, Mom. I'll talk to you . . . "

Mom grabbed my hand.

"Emmy?" She only called me that once before, when she told me she was pregnant with Chrissy. I couldn't imagine—yet had every idea—where she was going with this.

I looked into her sad eyes. Her normally porcelain face reflected no light, cracked gray. I forced a smile.

"Yeah, Ma?"

"I'm sorry if we haven't been good parents." Mom broke down.

What?! My soulheartbrain shattered in silent slo-mo.

"No, no, Mom! That's not it! You and Dad are great parents!" I started to cry again and took Mom's other hand.

Mom kept listening.

But I grabbed myself and calmed down: I couldn't tell her right now, not right after Pop's funeral. We were already too exhausted.

"I'm sorry I haven't been around much. I'll try to get home soon. I really love you, Mom." My waning sanity was going to explode if I did not escape. "I've gotta go."

Mom and I embraced once more, and I scrambled out of the car.

⚾ ⚾ ⚾

A SIMILARLY SAD PACKED SERVICE was held for Peter Pace two days later. None of this helped or mattered, more burlap death threads woven into my self-spun shroud.

⚾ ⚾ ⚾

OVER THE YEARS OF MY education, I kept hearing from teachers that the purpose of school was "to teach you how to question." But I had always taken things at face value, for two reasons—like a 1-2 punch:

1. All the questions had already been answered for me, thanks to the Church. I was taught how *not to* question authority, so I never learned *how to.*

2. I was raised to believe, and hence had a built in yen for believing. Which returns us to Item 1, above.

The negative effect of all this willfully ignorant believing—in the power of Love, final damnation, God's forgiveness—the psychocybernetic strength of my own mind —manifested itself in my inability NOT TO believe. To not believe what I had been taught. I had believed— never *questioned*—so much, for so long, that when I abruptly came up against the Big Question, and I came up with the "wrong" answer as the "right" answer, my psyche short-circuited.

I had believed in everything, and now that I could no longer, I suffered a Belief Gap, a vast space in my heartbrain where all those good things I had believed in could no longer live. In fact, they had already moved out. What to install in their absence? Since there was nothing left, there was nothing with which to fill the space.

In that instant choice, I had become empty. My heartbrain was numbly open and vacant. I was absent from myself. I could re-think none of my old thoughts, because they no longer existed, and so neither did I.

I wept in the coldness of all that room to think. A sublime terror: now, I was really on my own. The old coping devices—lighting a candle, going to Confession—were as empty as I was. I couldn't buy that voodoo anymore, and yet its deep inculcation, down to the roots of my soul, made it impossible for me to forgive myself my choice.

My parents' love for me was unconditional love, which said: So, you did that. What? I love you still.—So, what. They would forgive me.

Sadly, the Church's dogma now felt strictly conditional: If you do/not do this, then I will/will not love you.—If, then. And I had committed the big, unforgivable IF.

My unconscious, indoctrinated response was to excommunicate myself from my Self.

⚾ ⚾ ⚾

IN THE BLUES OFFICE LADIES' lounge, I rinsed my hands, then heard a flush and turned. Whitley emerged from the stall.

I dried my hands.

"Have you met the new ballgirl Liz yet, Mick?" Whitley asked. "She's really pretty and *so* nice."

I tossed the paper towel and proceeded to lipstick. Lipstick worn like so much war paint. Self-protective lipstick.

"Saw her down on the field Opening Day. Seemed OK."

"Well, you're not the only one who saw her. I heard she went out with Doug after the game." Whitley loved to get my goat, but she would never get my gossip.

"Good for her . . . I guess." I repursed my lipstick, turned on the water then realized I was washing my hands again. Out damn spot.

⚾ ⚾ ⚾

I INVITED MAGGIE TO GO with me to the team's season-opening charity event. I was obligated to attend, and she was always a good b.s. buffer.

Outside the Bingham-Stradley Hotel, Constitution Blues fans jammed the Centre Street sidewalk, waving team photos and pennants. Jack Black and his wife Candy emerged from a stretch limousine. Flashbulbs popped as they walked through the screaming crowd and into the hotel. This routine continued as Tommy Gunninski arrived with his Annie, Mark and Bobby rushed inside together, and Doug and Liz alighted from Doug's Corvette.

The night began with a team fashion show. Mark, aglow in a three-piece sharkskin suit, dance-strutted his way up the catwalk to Gloria Gaynor's "I Will Survive." We'll see about that.

Women crowded the stage and waved at Ridder. He turned stiffly, took off his jacket, then shook his bootie. The fanatics screamed with delight.

Doug and Liz sat with Glenn Goodall in a make-shift radio booth in a corner of the ballroom.

"Good evening, Folks! This is Glenn Goodall, and we're back, live from the Bingham-Stradley Grand Ballroom, where the Constitution Blues wives have put together yet another one of their outstanding Blue Balls to benefit testicular cancer research . . . "

Fans wearing team tees and jerseys crowded the booth. Maggie and I watched the commotion from a ringside table, as Goodall went on.

"We're here with the hottest young couple in baseball today, Doug Akins . . . "

"Howdy, folks."

"And the new Blues ballgirl, the lovely Liz."

"Hi-ii!" Liz squealed and beamed dizzily at Doug.

Maggie and I exchanged eyerolls at our corner table.

Glenn Goodall continued his interview.

"Now, the thing everyone wants to know is: what is your last name, Liz?"

"Well, it's going to be Akins! Isn't that all that really matters?"

I gripped Maggie's hand and felt the dizzying nausea of nothingness return.

"Did his divorce come through?" Maggie wondered aloud.

"I don't . . . let's go, Mags . . . take me home." This public display of Doug's new life hammered the final spike of humiliation into my psyche.

⚾ ⚾ ⚾

SOMEHOW I DRAGGED MY HOLLOW self into the office the next morning. Whitley was waiting for me.

"Have you heard the latest? Doug and Liz got engaged last night." She was squealing just like Liz had on the radio.

"Oh . . . I thought Doug was married." I played it off best I could, giving her more hand-washing nonchalance.

"I think his divorce came through a couple days ago."

I stood there, straight-faced, but I was certain I was blanching Bozo white.

"Some girls have all the luck," Whitley went on happily, "starts work one week, engaged to a Major Leaguer the next!"

I snapped out of my stupor.

"Yeah, well, he's playing like a minor leaguer, and the rest of the team's not doing so well either!"

Whitley stared at me, as Blake walked in.

I lowered my voice.

"In case you haven't noticed, Whitley, we're 1 and 8."

"Maybe it's some kind of home game jinx," Blake suggested, only half-kidding.

I gazed wide-eyed at Blake. Jinx, curse, whatever you wanted to call it, I was starting to think I had somehow brought it on. Me and my fraternizing.

There was an uncomfortable silence, then Blake added, "You know, with Peter and everything?" He chuckled but looked sketchy.

I realized I was staring at him. There I went again, my life as a movie, not living quite in it. I shook my head clear.

"I'm sorry, Blake, yeah . . . " I rubbed my brow. No way was I going to refute his home jinx theory. At least not out loud.

"Maybe they'll do better on the road . . . "

⚾ ⚾ ⚾

HOME, AWAY. AND ME: HOME and away, simultaneously. Hardly there at all yet standing right beside you belting the Anthem.

⚾ ⚾ ⚾

I WAS UNCERTAIN WHETHER I would ever feel like a good person again, regardless of what anyone else would ever say or even know.

The real mystery is how someone kind, good and moral could make what felt like a well-weighed and brave decision—given all considerations—taking one for "the team"—her other *family*, then turn and blame herself and feel herself to be none of these good things now that the deed was done. The doing of the deed, all preludes, understandings and contemplations aside, instantly relegated me to a place of unworthiness and judgment.

Stupid sluttiness.

I simply should have known better from the start. But I *did* know better from the start: Thou Shalt Not!

I should have paid closer attention to the practical things, then I would never have approached the awfulness.

But there I was and there I lay, fallow.

Studies of abortion patients have shown that their decision-making process before conception is often irrational. Even when informed, it is possible to be careless and forgetful. The erratic use of birth control is itself a decision—an irrational one, perhaps based on a subconscious desire to become pregnant.[†]

I knew how the plumbing worked but had neglected to install the correct filter, don the Tools of Ignorance before letting him slide home. If I had protected myself, that would have been too practical, premeditated: *prepared*. By that time I had been off Crayola-coloring Fantasyland, my Girl Scout badges back in Montgomery.

At the end of a troop meeting one night in the linoleum-tiled basement of the First Presbyterian Church, I lost my wind playing Red Rover. I thought I was going to die because, of course, I would never breathe again. Not the way it felt slab-cold on the tile under those fluorescent lights, them staring down, assuring me I would be all right, I had only just gotten the wind knocked out of me.

Now, I didn't *think* I was going to die. No, my anima, my life breath was gone, knocked out: I *was* dead.

⚾ ⚾ ⚾

BUT, OF COURSE, I WASN'T physically dead or even exactly out of breath, so I had to keep living somehow. Sometimes fairly often now and again the somehow was through sedation. I smoked more often, even before work.

One day in the office, Hugh Sargent asked me whether I had had any Buds lately.

"Buds? Hugh?" I figured he meant the beer, or at least would assume so til he said otherwise. He had seen me in the Press Club after games, so what gave?

"I think we should go out sometime, you and I, Mick."

A date? Oh, God! It is so awkward when guys you like want to date you.

"Yeah, but, Hugh, I mean, is this a date?"

"No, Mick, as buds."

"Oh, OK, yeah, great."

He gives me the try not to look so relieved look.

"I mean, 'cause you're my pal, but I'm not really *dating* right now."

"No? You, Mick?"

No, just fucking mostly. (Ouch.)

"Nah, I'm just—uh—so when should we go out?"

"Team's out of town next Tuesday and there's no moon—perfect for stargazing."

After work Tuesday, Hugh drove me uptown to Cobblestone for beers and bites, then we headed to Fortside Hill State Park with Hugh's telescope—and a mutual pledge not to listen to the game. Sometimes you just have to give it a rest.

"So, Babe, now that I have you out here in the park in the dark . . . " He reached under his seat.

"Yes, Doctor Seuss?"

"What's your sign?" He packed some green into a pipe.

"Oh, that would be hit-and-run, *Bud*." He knew nothing of my recent accident.

"No, Mick, really, what's your star sign?" He lit up.

"That would be Moon Child, or as the traditionalists would have it, Cancer."

"Crab! I shoulda known!" Ha ha. "Do you know about the Crab Nebula?" God, he was so excited, waved the pipe and a spark jumped onto the floorboard. He chuckled and stomped it out.

"Um, no. Here, give that to me." I took a hit. "Tasty."

"Yeah, it's pretty good. I like to treat myself after a hard day at the yard."

"Oh, yeah, like you're Fred Flintstone at the quarry!"

"Those free Buds in the Press Club can't light my fire the way some nice tea can. And they want to do testing. I say start with a breathalyzer on all of 'em."

"Yeah, I'm still waiting to hear about a stoner driving into a streetlamp." [†]

"You'll never hear that, they're driving too slowly to veer off too quickly in any one direction!" We cracked ourselves up.

"So, what's with the Crab Nebula?"

"Here, let's find it." He positioned the telescope. "Here! Look!"

I put my eye to the small end of the tube.

"In the center of the Crab Nebula is a pair of stars, one of which is an imposter which flashes 30 times a second. For a long while, because the only photos of the Crab were time-lapsed, it appeared there was a steady pair of stars at its center. In 1969—69 by chance the zodiac symbol for Cancer," he nudged me, "they finally took a series of snapshots, which revealed the flashing nature of the imposter star. The Crab was created by a supernova explosion seen and recorded by Chinese astronomers on about July 4, 1054." [†]

"I got yer fireworks right here! Cool!"

"Can I kiss you now?"

I gasped.

"Just kidding, Mick! Relax, would you?"

I sighed. If only I could tell him. But what would I say? What could be said?

"I wonder if the imposter would ever just flicker out and not come back on?"

Hugh took me home, a friendly hug goodnight. Hugh was a little too real for me right then, so close to knowing me in a non-verbal way that I thereafter politely avoided him—grateful to him from afar, trying not to flicker out.

I entered the apartment to find Carly slouched on the couch, TV tuned to the Blues. Glenn Goodall announced, " . . . and that's the game." Another loss.

"I feel like such a liar," I said, "telling all those season ticket holders how good we were going to be. That was really bad karma—we suck!"

"It's not your fault, Mick."

"Yeah, but these guys aren't just losing. They aren't even scoring except when Jack dings one."

"Maybe Slug lost his lucky jock strap. Or maybe Fizz shrank it."

I smiled and rolled my eyes at Carly, appreciating her what-the-hex support. But I was pretty convinced of my shaky best effort and its curse-yielding fallout.

⚾ ⚾ ⚾

MEANWHILE, POST-GAME, BLUES MANAGER TEDDY Mack stood in the middle of the visitors' clubhouse as the players peeled off their muddy uniforms.

"Fellas, you really stunk it up tonight! I see no concentration in the field or at the plate, and every time we get close, we blow it! Would anyone care to explain this for me?"

Problem is, when you're losing, there is no real explanation. But they were willing to try.

"Well, Skip, I switched brands of dip when we left on the road trip," Mark offered.

Mack stared at Ridley.

Jack Black attempted a more traditional guise.

"What he meant to say, Coach, is that we have a young team."

"We have to make a few adjustments, that's all." Doug added analysis straight from the Sports page, those 'few adjustments.'

"These guys just have to adjust to the bigs. They'll be all right," Tommy said.

"They seem like they're *adjusting* just fine, Gunner." Mack looked at Doug.

"They certainly haven't been making curfew!"

Doug turned back to his locker.

"Sorry, Skip," Bobby said, "I got a late call from the coast last night . . . "

Mack rolled his eyes, when will these boys ever learn?

" . . . from my mom, she found my old glove! It should be at the stadium tomorrow."

"As should my order of new bats," said Jack.

"Don't forget to spit on 'em, JB," Moss muttered under his breath. Moss was a spitter.

"Fellas! I don't think it's an equipment problem. Please get your heads into the game!" Mack's tone dropped.

"Get showered. We depart at 11:30."

⚾ ⚾ ⚾

THE CONSTITUTION BLUES PLAYERS, COACHES and traveling personnel walked out onto the tarmac and boarded the team charter in the dark, heavy rain. Take-off went without a hitch, but the climb was rough. After the plane leveled off, the stewardesses served cocktails.

Jack Black and Doug sat playing backgammon. Doug made his move as the plane bounced.

"Whoa, Mama!" said Jack.

"Good move, huh?" said Doug.

"No, Smug, I meant the turbulence."

"No wonder we can't win," Doug teased loudly, "our home run champ is a wimp!"

Tommy Gunn and Ridder, sitting two rows behind, looked up from their card game.

"Look, Akins," Tommy said, "just because you scored that ballgirl . . . "

" . . . not to mention your *teammate* Mick." Ridder said, pouring it on.

As Bobby looked up from his book and across the aisle at Ridder, the plane was hit by lightning, dropping several feet. Oxygen masks sprang from their overhead stow bins. Everyone gasped, grabbing for armrests. Drinks, cards and backgammon chips tumbled. Some guys tried to put on their air masks. Then, just as suddenly, the plane steadied, and they regrouped, brushing off their imminent demise.

Doug turned around in his seat. Bobby was staring at him over the top of his book.

⚾ ⚾ ⚾

BUCK WEAVER, THE SOLE MEMBER of the 1919 Chicago Black Sox who refused to take part in the plot, was with his teammates banned from baseball under Major League Baseball Rule 21: *because he didn't reveal their conspiracy.*[†] The biblical roots are clear: the corollary to the Ninth Commandment is that we are called to speak truthfully, that silence in the face of vice is as ruinous as bearing false witness.

⚾ ⚾ ⚾

THOUGH I HAD CHOSEN TO remain silent and not burden Kelly with the Doug story, I nonetheless relied on her friendship and humor through my self-contained suffering, and frequented the switchboard during my breaks.

I leaned forward on the reception desk as Kelly hung up the phone.

"Can you believe Mr. Preston OK'd a budget for the shower? Brought to you by the Knot-Hole Gang!" The Blues had continued their losing ways and box seat sales were way down.

I shook my head.

"At this point, I'd believe anything . . . if there's anything left to believe in."

The switchboard rang again as Whitley got off the elevator.

Kelly answered, "Constitution Blues, may I help you?" She rolled her eyes at me and raised her voice. "Hello, Blues?!"

She hung up the phone and turned to me and Whitley.

"They wanted the mortuary."

Kelly and I share a we're pathetic giggle.

Whitley drew a blank, so, apropos of nothing, proudly announced, "Well, I've already called the caterer. It shouldn't be too expensive, I told him nothing elaborate."

Kelly and I exchanged looks as Whitley worked her fantasy by proxy.

"They make such a great couple . . . Liz will be such a beautiful bride." She exhaled, "Isn't it exciting, a baseball wedding! It's like a fairytale . . . "

⚾ ⚾ ⚾

LATE THAT EVENING CARLY LAY on the couch reading, when I entered the apartment, Budweiser bulldozer incarnate. I slammed the door.

"They make SUCH a great couple . . . Liz will be SUCH a beautiful bride . . . "

Carly sat up, concerned.

My eyes welled as I ranted on.

"Isn't it exCIting, a baseball wedding, it's like a FAIrytale!" I broke down sobbing.

Carly rushed over and put her arm around me. She wasn't much of a hugger.

"I don't know how you stand it, Mick. They would die if they had any idea." She pulled a tissue from the box on the end table and handed it to me. I angrily wiped my tears.

"It's all I can do not to just puke right in their faces! I really don't know how much longer I can hack it, Car." I bawled.

"You should just quit, Mick. You could get a job anywhere. Who needs it?"

I shook my head.

"Yeah, but if I quit, everyone will think it's because we're losing!"

Carly screwed up her face and shook her head at me:

> There is, however, a limit at which forbearance
> ceases to be a virtue.[†]

My thoughts were rotting driftwood, and what I needed was ash. Real winners never cheat; therefore, I was not a real winner, might as well quit. Though cheaters can win, perhaps, in the short run, quitters can *never* win. I couldn't quit. But, I cheated, I must pay. I must quit.

" . . . then again, that's why I have to quit." I dropped to the couch and buried my head in my hands.

Carly sat down next to me and grabbed the remote, clicked the TV on.

"Don't start with the karma crap again, Mick. It's not your fault. You're too superstitious."

On the TV screen, Dionne Warwick's face came into focus.

"Here, at the Psychic Friends Network . . . "

I WANTED TO READ GOD'S mind. How *does* free will exist alongside His plan for your life? By exerting your God-given free will into said plan for your life, do you not create a negative absolute value situation: your free will is/becomes God's plan for your life, and you are thus ever free in your free will—free to feel forgiven even?

But where does that leave "*God's* will be done?" How often in a moment, then, might the exertion of one's free will manifest itself in plain old, never-to-be-blamed-on-God bad luck?

THEY WERE LOSING. I HAD to quit.

THE BUMS, FULL MOON FEVER
& PANDORA'S BOX

*Many a long dispute among divines may be thus
abridged: It is so. It is not so. It is so. It is not so.[†]*

A fter more internal coin-tossing, I arranged to speak
with Mr. Preston after lunch. "Thanks for . . . "

"Yes, Mick, what is it? I don't have a lot of time.
I've got to get back to Metro about that trade."

"Well, I know my timing's not the greatest, but, well,
here's my letter of resignation."

Preston looked up from his stat sheets.

"Mary Katharine, I'm surprised. I thought you were a
lifer. We're going to miss you."

"You know I'll miss you too, Mr. Preston. You've been
. . . really great to me." I struggled not to cry.

"Well, let me know if you need a recommendation. You're
not bad—for a girl." Of course, he was kidding me, but that was
just the problem, my female troubles. But I couldn't tell him
that, no sir, that wasn't team business, that was my own red E.

"Thanks, but I've already got something lined up."
My eyes welled. I wondered whether my hormones
would *ever* regulate! I gulped a little and tried to get
a grip.

"You know I'll never stop rooting for the team."
True, but.

"Well, best of luck to you, Mary Katharine."

Preston rose and shook my hand.

"Thanks. You too, Mr. Preston."

I took a deep breath and held my game face. I opened
the door to Suzanne's outer office, leaving it ajar.

Suzanne looked up as I passed through and out into
the hallway in a rudderless drift. She shrugged, took an
emery board from beneath the papers on her desk and
filed away.

⚾ ⚾ ⚾

Later that afternoon, I walked down the aisle to the
back table of the Continental Diner, where a Santa-faced
man of about 75 sat working a crossword puzzle.

"Can I take your order, sir?"

The man indicated the TV.

"Yes, can you please get our team a win? The bums!"

I smiled at him: the bums! Then I spotted his faded cap
with the fancy C under *The Almanack*. I couldn't help
myself—but added an 's' out of respect.

"Wish I could, Pops. Unfortunately, that doesn't seem to
be on the menu."

> *I dreamed there would be Spring no more,*
> *That Nature's ancient power was lost.*[†]

Back at home, I stuffed myself into the couch, head inside
"The Summer Game."

Carly muttered from behind her *Rolling Stone*. "You see this? Some chick calling herself 'Madonna' getting the Catholics all hot and bothered."

The phone rang. Carly and I exchanged looks. I got the phone.

"Hi, Mom . . . Sorry I didn't call you back yesterday. I was on late shift, and by the time I . . . It's OK . . . Yeah, I heard. Those guys can't buy a win . . . Saturday?" I looked over at Carly.

"Oh, no, I promised Car I'd take the bus to Chance with her Saturday."

Carly looked up from her magazine.

". . . I know . . . Well, Joe's birthday is coming up, I'll definitely make that . . . I'm sorry, Mom . . . I miss you too. Bye."

Before I had the phone on the hook, Carly was on me.

"So, who's bankrolling the trip to "Chance"?!"

"It was the quickest thing I could think of, Carly!"

Chance, short for Enchanted City, had only recently begun casting its die on the Constitution gamblers. I had discovered this while researching competitive entertainment for Mr. Preston just before I quit. It wouldn't be expensive: we could take the Harvey's Casino bus and get the fare back in quarters for slots, plus a buffet dinner—if we went, that is.

"Well, stop including me in your façade, Mick! You can't keep ignoring it, it won't go away!"

Nietzsche proposed *amor fati*,[†] the love of one's fate, those chance happenings: if you say 'no' to a single factor in your life, you unravel the whole thing, it *will* go away. *Had* gone away?

"Look, all I'm trying to do right now is make it through each day, OK?"

⚾ ⚾ ⚾

I know not whether Laws be right,
Or whether Laws be wrong;
All that we know who lie in gaol
Is that the wall is strong;
And that each day is like a year,
A year whose days are long.[†]

The Blues sales staff bled along with their lost teammate, its days long.

"That's about the tenth call I've had today from someone asking for Mick," said Whitley.

"I never realized how many season tickets she sold," said Blake.

"Well, lucky her," said Whitley. "She's not here to listen to them all complain now."

"Complain? I had three this morning demand their money back!" Blake said.

⚾ ⚾ ⚾

THE LOSSES ACCRUED. MANAGER TEDDY Mack slumped in the chair across from Preston's desk, post-game. He knew what was coming: baseball as usual.

"I feel that I have no alternative, Mack . . . " Like a bad pitch to the skull.

". . . I didn't want you to read it in the papers."

"I understand, Lloyd." Pinch runner takes first.

"You're a good man, Mackie, but we've just got to do something with these youngsters before the All-Star break, or we'll be saying 'next year' come July."

"I just wish I could have helped them. They're not THIS bad, are they?"

⚾ ⚾ ⚾

I swept the floor of the Continental. "Pops," the old Blues fan, sat at his back table with his newspapers. He held up the *Daily View.*

"See that, Miss? Three in a row." Yeah, I had noticed.

"Maybe they just needed a new manager. Then again, it's not like they just swept the Dockers."

The Dockers were the perennial West division champs and had won three pennants in recent seasons. Their home park was the Disneyland of Baseball: everything was perfect from the weather to the hotdog guy's baritone to the surgery-sculpted face on the fan down the row. But they were not the Blues' true rivals. We would have to get past the Metro Swingers if we wanted to make the playoffs.

> *The boisterous Sea of Liberty*
> *is never without a wave.*[†]

A couple wins, the baseball gods threw us a curveball. At Pembroke Hospital, Dr. Howard Preston gingerly examined the middle finger of Jack Black's right hand.

Jack gestured wildly with his left.

"But, you don't know my mother-in-law!"

The Blues' new manager, Skip Healey, a silver-fox affably pot-bellied man, leaned on the exam table.

"I don't care if it was your friggin patron saint! How's it look, Doc?"

"It's all the way down to the bone," Doc Preston said. "He'll have to sit out for at least four weeks. We'll reevaluate in two."

Healey gritted his teeth and inhaled. Jack on the DL would put everybody's bats into a coma, just when they had begun reviving.

Doc Preston guided him to a chair and sat him down.

"I'll call Lloyd."

Doc left the room.

Jack and Healey exchanged somber looks.

At Liberty Stadium, the phone rang in Lloyd Preston's office, where he and Blake Bedford reviewed the Blues ticket sales reports, two cock-eyed optimists.

"A few more wins, they'll come back," said Preston.

"Yeah, it's not like these guys aren't good or anything," Blake agreed.

Preston picked up his big black phone.

"Well, hello, brother Howard! . . . WHAT?!"

Preston's and Blake's eyes locked. Preston's bulged.

"He what?! Who pays his damn salary, anyway?! . . . "

Blake diverted his gaze. His eyes fell on the dusty trophy on Preston's shelf. He looked down, then jumped as Preston yelled again.

"Give these guys a damn day off, and look what happens! So much for that three game win 'streak!' . . . I know, Howard . . . Ow!"

Preston grimaced and clutched his beltline.

Blake quickly got up and moved toward him.

Preston swatted him away.

" . . . Mylanta. Thanks, Howard. And tell Jack-the-Clipper he can do the damn hedges out front of the stadium while he's on the DL!"

Preston slammed down the receiver and grabbed his stomach.

Blake slinked out of the office.

Back at Pembroke Hospital, Skip Healey grunted at Jack Black.

"Your mother-in-law?" Skip looked at him sideways.

Jack nodded sheepishly.

"She single?"

⚾ ⚾ ⚾

A WEEK LATER, I CHANNEL surfed, prostrate on the couch, playing potato those days when not slinging them. (I was such a quitter.) I stopped at a rerun of "The Brady Bunch." It was the one where Marcia had the crush on the quarterback.

The phone rang. I looked at the clock on the kitchen wall: 2:30. I slumped further into the couch, staring at the TV. The phone rang again. I rolled over and buried my head in the throw pillows. The phone rang a third time. I popped up off the couch and grabbed it.

"Hello."

"Mick, it's Kelly."

"Oh—Kell. Hi. What's up?"

"I just wanted to say hi, see how you were. We really miss you around here . . . you didn't even tell me . . . "

I interrupted before Kelly asked for The Truth, because I would have to tell her if she asked.

"I miss you too, Kel, but it's not like I was a home run champ who retired. Or sliced his finger."

"Isn't it awful? We haven't won a game since!"

"I know, Kel. I can't really stay on right now, but I'll talk to ya, OK? Thanks for calling me. Bye."

I hung up the phone and looked over at the TV: Marcia had suffered her fateful swollen nose and couldn't go to the dance with the football player.

I closed my eyes then rubbed my nose a sec: Pinocchio! (Not just a quitter, a liar.)

I rushed the coffee table, grabbed the remote and resumed channel surfing. I stopped at the game.

Glenn Goodall informed me that "on this beautiful Sunday afternoon at Downey Stadium, it's 2-1 Blues after two," over a shot of a dad shouldering his blond toddler, who smiled and waved a Blues pennant.

I flopped back down on the couch.

"Too early, kid." I clicked the game off. I started to weep, quietly at first. Sobs gradually wracked my body into its fetal position.

⚾ ⚾ ⚾

A FULL MOON HUNG OVER Liberty Stadium like a big, mottled baseball. The division-leading arch rival Metro Swingers were that night's opponents, and many away fans wore their team on their sleeves and their red and maroon painted faces. The sellout crowd was abuzz, filling the stadium in waves of freshly pulled beer, a tad foamy on top. The Bluesman circled the field on his motortrike. Banners read: "SMASH THE SWINGAS!," "WHACK IT OFF, JACK?" and "WHO'S YOUR BUDDY?" It would not take long for high tide to arrive.

The fans' rivalry found its voice with the player introductions. Duke Braun wrapped the Swingers' line-up over the PA.

"Pitching and batting ninth . . . Number Thirty-Three . . . Duck-yyy Hooperrr . . . "

The Swinger fans hooted and whooped for their favorite flake.

"Go, Ducky!" "Atta boy, Ducky!" "Hoop! Hoop! Hoop!"

The Bluesman pulled his arms up to his sides and waddled down the third base line past the visiting dugout.

The Blues fans shouted and laughed.

"Quack, quack!" "I shoulda bought my shotgun! Ha, Ha!"

Some Swinger fans glared in the direction of the Bluesman, while others threw their dirty looks at the home fans.

"Don't worry about it, we'll whip yer butts on da field!" "What's that stupit lookin blue thing?" "How stupit!"

" . . . and the manager of the Swingers, Buddy Cross," announced Duke Braun.

The Bluesman bashed an effigy of Buddy Cross with a groundskeeping hoe, then voodoo danced around it.

The Blues fans cheered their approval.

"We're gonna beat 'em today, I just feel it!" "C'mon, you guys!" "Go, Blues!"

The Swinger fans were tired of the Bluesman.

"Let's get on wit it!" "Get that stupit blue thing off da field!" "Start da game already!"

The Bluesman mounted his motortrike, ran over "Buddy Cross," and rode off the field.

The Blues fans went nuts. The PA crackled.

"Ladies and Gentlemen, please rise as we honor America with the playing of our National Anthem."

The crowd reverently rose, fellow statesmen all. The rivalry resumed quickly with the first pitch, however.

The Swinger fans yelled: "Let's go, Ducky!" "Let's go, Swinggaas!"

The Blues fans came back: "Strike 'em out, Bobby!" "Mow 'em down, Bobby!" "Bahn-son! Bahn-son!"

The fans got increasingly rowdy as the game progressed, enjoying damning their rivals nearly as much as cheering their idols.

But be careful, sinners: obsession with your rival is reverse idolatry; and since your rival is the sporting devil incarnate, you thereby idolize the devil, even as you demonize him!

Bobby threw well, and the back and forth went on. But when he ran into trouble in the seventh, letting in three, the Swinger fans cut loose.

"Ha, ha, who's laughin' now?" "A three run lead'll hold you guys!" "Yeah, they nevva score moah than three inna game anyway!" "Yeah, specially since Black's mother-in-law trimmed their offense!!" "HA, HA!!"

At the encouragement of the Bluesman, the homers started The Wave whooo-ing its way around the Lib. There goes The Wave, and again: the fans' synchronicity would spark a rally, they just knew it!

"No batta, no batta, no batterrrr!!!"

But, as The Wave circled the stadium, a home fan collided with a visiting fan. Tempers flared, and a fight broke out between the rivals, as Ridley was called from the pen with a man on second and two out.

More fans joined the melee, and Blues security guards attempted to intervene.

At home I heard Glenn Goodall's play-by-play in stereo. Carly and I couldn't afford cable to get the home games, so I caught the Blues on the radio when they played in Constitution. I really missed the scene at the Lib. But tonight?

"Half the upper deck is in a frenzy! Heh, the fans sure are having trouble maintaining their good sportsmanship tonight! We'll be right back. 6-3 Swingers. Now a word from Anheuser-Busch."

"Carly! Did you hear that? There's a big fight going on at the Lib!"

Carly ran in from her bedroom.

"What'd they say?"

"Swingers-Blues, full moon . . . " I said. "They're wasted!"

⚾ ⚾ ⚾

Back at Liberty Stadium, a body fell from the upper deck and fans below reeled in horror. The EMTs rushed to the scene with their stretcher and tool kit.

The ramps jammed with fleeing fans as Mark Ridley's first pitch was hit for a two-run homer. He struck out Ducky

Hooper and walked to the dugout, chucking his glove on the bench.

The few remaining fans, as at a spottily attended service, moved down front, closer to the field. They stretched perfunctorily mid-seventh inning.

The Seventh Inning Stretch is like the Sign of Peace at Mass: by now you should have greeted your neighbor-fans, perhaps even shared sustenance with them—bread & wine or hotdogs & beer (just not before the second inning, that could be Anacreonistic). But there was no peace at the Lib tonight.

" . . . if they don't win, it's a shame . . . "

It was a shame, and the Constitution Blues fans booed loudly as they exited the stadium to the taunts of the Swinger fans.

"Ha, ha! Better luck next year!!!"

Carly and I sat in the living room, listening to the post-game show, sharing a joint. I took a hit as Glenn Goodall continued on the radio.

" . . . An eventful evening here at the Lib . . . eight runs, twelve hits, no errors for the visiting Swingers; three runs, four hits, three errors for the Blues."

I slowly blew smoke.

"Hooper gets the win, the L goes to Bahnson."

I took another hit and held my breath, passed the j to Carly.

"For those of you who are wondering, the fan who fell from the upper deck is in critical condition at Pembroke Hospital, but he is expected to make it."

I choked as I exhaled.

"Expected to *make it*! This is nuts!" I shook my head. "That's the last thing they needed."

Carly exhaled, then toked again, croaked over her exhale.

"Nothing like a PR problem to take your mind off your team's record."

I gestured at Carly to pass the joint.

⚾ ⚾ ⚾

THE MORNING DAWNED DARKLY. GUSTING winds whipped trash around Constitution Hall courtyard, Liberty Stadium barely visible down Centre Street.

In the Blues conference room, the front office staff sat in silent vigil sipping coffee. Hugh Sargent contemplated periodic ophthalmia and its effect on batting averages. Blake and Whitley straggled in just ahead of Lloyd Preston.

"I imagine you've all read today's Sports."

He held up a copy of the *Daily View*. The headline blared: "FULL MOON FULL GAINER; FULL LOSERS," and a pair of photos showed the fan in mid-fall and then being stretchered into the ambulance.

The staffers shifted in their seats. Preston went on.

"The suggestion box is officially opens, folks. I'm not throwing in the towel, but we have a real bear on our hands, and at this point, anything goes. Let's brainstorm."

Whitley whispered to Blake in the corner.

"I just hope that guy makes it."

"Shut up, Whitley," Blake whispered back. "That's no hitter talk."

"What do you mean?"

"Will you NEVER get it? It's like a no hitter in the making: you can hope for it, but whatever you do, *don't talk about it*!"

She still looked confused, so Blake paraphrased.

"We ALL hope he makes it."

Mr. Preston overheard Blake and Whitley's sidebar.

"Whitley, dear, let me put it in terms you'll understand. The All-Star break is next week, and we're just about mathematically eliminated. That means we don't go to the playoffs, no World Series . . . "

And Blake added, "Which means no rings, no bonuses, no nothing, Whitley."

"Oh. Desperation time."

The assembled troops aimed eyeballs heavenward.

"Shut up, Whitley! We could still do it."

Blake looked around for reassurance. Everybody else was pretty damn quiet.

⚾ ⚾ ⚾

IT STARTED TO DRIZZLE. I paid the corner paperman for *The Almanack* and opened to Sports.

The headline read: "DID FAN FALL OR JUMP?" over a photo of last night's full moon. Should've gone up to the roof and held up a BIG bag, I thought.

Rain now in full drop, I covered my head with the paper and broke into a trot.

I entered the empty Continental, shook the rain from my jacket and hung it on the coat rack. I approached the back table holding up *The Almanack*.

"Pops! You see this?!"

Pops looked up from his crossword and gestured with his pencil. Of course he had.

"If I'da been there I mighta jumped too, Mick! Boy, do those bums look lousy!"

I tied on my apron and pulled a pad of checks from my pocket, felt around for something to write with.

"C'mon, Bobby hung tight 'til the seventh."

"Yeah, but that Akins sure blew that long ball. AND that throw to the plate."

Pops handed me his pencil. I nodded and smiled.

"Yeah. I hope that guy gets better . . . The fan, I mean."

I brought Pops his usual: "Scrambled eggs, the home fries and that scrapple. And your awful coffee, of course."

"Looks like they're gettna break tonight, anyway." Rain beat against the plate glass and lightning shot through the patchy dark clouds.

I stared out at the sky, listening to the rumbling, feeling it in my bones.

I walked to the pay phone but paused, hand on receiver.

> 'Tis not in the power of England or Europe
> to conquer America, if she does not conquer
> herself by delay and timidity.[†]

Another bolt, closer now. Thunder rattled the windows.

I unhooked the phone, slotted a quarter and dialed.

"Constitution Blues, can I help you?"

"Kel, it's me. Sorry I was short the other day."

"Yeah, Carmel, I was only trying to be a friend . . . Are you O-K?"

"I'm OK. How's Mr. P. holding up?"

"Not so great. It was a real nightmare last night. Everybody's really depressed. We need a miracle or the fat lady's gonna break into *I Am Your Spaniel* any minute."

"I have to see him."

"What's going on, Mick? Are you *really* OK?" I couldn't blame her for being suspicious. I had left the team rather abruptly—without explanation.

"I can explain, Kel, I promise. I just have to speak to the Big Mahoff first."

"Okay, if you say so, but you're still a big weirdo."

A pair of wet and hungries walked in the door past me.

"Oh, shit, Kel, gotta go. I'll call you later."

I hustled to the table where the new patrons had parked. I half-smiled in apology.

"What'll it be?" A championship? Sure, no problem!

⚾ ⚾ ⚾

In revenge for Prometheus's stealing his fire, Zeus created a woman to whom the gods gave all the gifts: Beauty, Grace, Wit, Melody and so on; she was called Pandora, "all-gifted." Zeus presented Pandora to Epimetheus as a wife, and Epimetheus took her—despite Prometheus's warning against gifts from Zeus. With Pandora came a box which she was forbidden to open, but she just couldn't help herself: out of the box flew the spirits of Death, Old Age, Famine, Sickness, Grief—and all the plagues of humanity![†]

Fortunately, Hope remained at the bottom of Pandora's box. Only the spirit of Hope could ever sustain humans under the weight of life's ills. After my Pandora experience, Hope was all my defiant self had left.

⚾ ⚾ ⚾

Shift over, I exited the Continental and sprinted the two blocks home holding my jacket over my head, my arms in its sleeves. I was smiling and felt like an angel, flapping my wings as I puddle-jumped the crosswalks.

I entered the apartment, soaked. Breathing quickly, I dialed the phone.

"Suzanne, it's Mick Carmichael. Is Mr. Preston still there?"

"He's a little tied up, Mary Katharine," Suzanne sighed. "Is there a message?" She asked as though she wasn't interested and doubted I had anything important to say. As usual.

"Does he have time to see me tomorrow?" I could hear her eyes roll through the receiver. "I promise it'll be short and sweet."

"Hold on, I'll check his schedule."

Suzanne may have been annoyed, but she also knew the boss liked me.

Then again, I was left on hold listening to Blues sound bites for what seemed like two decades.

"Another home run! Akins is bound for the Hall if he keeps this up!"

I pursed my lips when I heard Glenn's pronouncement—what?

Carly walked in, waved hello and went to the fridge.

I danced around, keeping the phone to my ear.

"What a March this youngster's having . . . " Oh, a Spring Training replay! Then, a click.

"Still there?"

Finally!

"Still here . . . " Carly turned from the fridge and looked at me.

"Six o'clock in his box."

"Six o'clock, in his box. Thanks, Suzanne . . . " I hung up and made a funny face at Carly. " . . . You're terrific!"

Carly grabbed and jostled me.

"No, Mick, you are!"

I hugged Carly thanks, then detached and gave her a we'll see look.

> *But what about chance? Is there anything in your life that did not occur as by chance? . . . Chance, or what might seem to be chance, is the means through which life is realized. The problem is not to blame or explain but to handle the life that arises . . . take it all as if it had been of your intention—with that, you evoke the participation of your will.*[†]

SUPERSTITIOUS BASEBALL PEOPLE, A TRADE & BEST EFFORTS

Superstition sets the whole world in flames;
Philosophy quenches them.[†]

I paused in the doorway of the Owner's Box, inhaled deeply and checked the view. God, how I loved it: all that greenness, the sounds of salt & pepper, the murmur of early arrivers, the pops from the batting cage followed by caroms off the outfield wall.

Mr. Preston looked up from his binoculars and greeted me with a forced-hearty smile.

"Mary Katharine, it's been a while!"

I descended the turf-carpeted steps and shook Mr. Preston's hand.

"Hey, Mr. Preston!"

I sat down and we turned to look at batting practice, a moment of silence.

I spotted Doug leaning on the cage. Time to leap.

"I wish things were going better for you guys."

Preston shook his head and sighed, his false heartiness displaced by honest despair.

"Yes, thanks." He then half smiled, offering what good news he could.

"Things are looking up, the fan . . . " His face darkened again.

"Well, of course you heard . . . "

I nodded. Heard? I'll never forget hearing Glenn's coverage of the frenzy on the radio. It got my attention, it got me where I was, to that exact moment.

"He's improving steadily . . . "

Suddenly Mr. Preston grabbed his side and his face became one of horror-lined disgust. He looked like he might vomit.

"It is our record I'm most concerned with at the moment."

My moment.

"That is your job, ultimately, Mr. Preston, but . . . well, that's why I came to see you. I want to help you."

Preston smiled at my offer and closed his eyes.

I took a quiet deep breath and continued, serious as a kid on a dare.

"I've watched this team all season. I think I can shed some light on their poor performance."

"Well, Mick," Preston chuckled and sat up. "That's VERY nice of you, but I have men here whom I pay a lot of money to *shed light* for me. What else?"

He turned back to his binoculars.

"What else? I'm serious. I think I can . . . please, if I may, I mean, I know I'm a girl and everything, but they say women are intuitive, don't they?"

Preston turned back to me.

"I don't know the first blasted thing about women!"

I held my earnest gaze on Mr. Preston.

"If I didn't like you, Mary Katharine . . . Go ahead."

I plunged in.

"Are you superstitious?"

Preston slapped his hand to his forehead.

"Hell, Mick, aren't all baseball people superstitious? Please, go on!"

"I have reason to believe there's bad blood on the team."

"*Bad blood*?"

"Well, bad karma. Do you know about karma?"

Preston stared at me as if I had completely lost my mind, and started to rise.

I grabbed his hand and looked him straight in the eye. *Bless me, father, for I have sinned.*

"Mr. Preston, there's a curse on your team." Now I had his attention.

He sat back down.

"You know, the first time you called me to your office, I was certain you were going to fire me, and then you hired me. Last time I came to see you, I guess I surprised you when I resigned, supposedly because I had this other job."

I shook my head.

"I had no other job. I have been waitressing at the Continental Diner. I left because I felt I had brought bad luck to the team."

Preston looked at me sideways. I pressed on.

"You know: Peter's parachute, then the team charter got hit by lightning, they were playing stupid-badly."

Preston cringed, so I moved on.

"But you were right. I AM a lifer, I love the team more than anything, and nothing changed after I left! In fact, things got worse: Jack's accident, and then with the fallen fan . . . I had to come back to let you know, to change the luck."

I was sure I sounded crazy.

Mr. Preston cleared his throat.

"What is it I have to know?"

Thank God, he was still with me.

"Well, let's say, um, well, I—uh."

How the hell . . . how much did he need to know? I had tried to rehearse this, but.

"I want my job back, and . . . No, actually, I want to work for YOU."

His open look relaxed me a bit.

"You know I've got great *stuff*," I smiled, "and, well, um, I think we need to make a trade."

What, her faith for my doubt? Preston was transfixed.

"A trade?"

"It wasn't me bringing the team down."

I paused again, Preston waited, I grimaced.

"Oh, God! I *fraternized* with D-A, and it went really . . . "

I shook my head and turned away—quick!—before I lost my game face. I swallowed hard and stared across the field into the void.

"Not well," Preston saved me.

"No, not well."

I shut my eyes: fuck Frankie Valli, I wanted to cry in this flash of the emptiness! But the crack of a bat brought me back: I realized I was done crying. The ball soared over the wall.

I looked at Mr. Preston once more and cleared my throat.

"I had to let you know what happened, so we can win again."

Preston patted me on the hand and stood up.

"Well, now we've some work to do."

I brightened to hear him say 'we've.'

"Nine sharp tomorrow." He gave me the nod.

⚾ ⚾ ⚾

THE EL PULLED IN, AND the conductor barked. "Constitution Hall, free interchange to the Centre Street Line, trolley numbers 13, 23 . . . " I alighted from the El and headed to the Centre Street Line. I was dressed in a double-breasted suit, hose and heels, and my make-up and hair were perfect. Passing riders watched me as I glided through the interchange and down the steps onto the platform. I felt like Cinderella—on my way to The Ball, yo.

I stood on the Southbound platform and looked impatiently up the track. I checked out the other travellers, in particular a young woman a few yards away who rocked her baby swaddled in blue, calming him. The woman caught me looking at her. I quickly smiled at her, and she nodded.

I noticed a guy standing on the far end of the platform. He was sporting in his minor league beer gut, navy blazer and gray trousers. He leaned his thin portfolio against his leg and opened his newspaper, tabloid fold. Must be the *Daily View*.

I idly read the billboards across the tracks: Parkham Junior College, the Y, The Camera Crop, Silver Sparrow Adoptions. I took a deep breath at that last one.

The subway rushed into the station, obscuring the ads. I looked back at the young woman and her baby, stepped onto the train and chose a seat near the doors.

The platform guy walked through the connecting door from the next car. I noticed his tie was loose, his blazer a little linty and his khakis somewhat rumpled. As he passed, our eyes met.

Though the car was somewhat vacant, the rider returned and sat down in front of me and opened his paper. After a minute, the train tugged out of the station.

As the subway symphony reached full crescendo, I leaned forward and snuck a peek at the guy's *Daily View*. My eyes bugged and an involuntary grin creased my face.

I got lost in thought. Maybe they *will* start to win again.

The rider, who had noticed me leaning up behind him, turned his head half over his shoulder. He smacked the paper, yelling to be heard over the din of the subway.

"See that?!"

I jumped out of my daydream.

"Finally!! They sent Akins back down on the farm where he belongs!"

I smiled and leaned up again, then shouted back.

"Well, the Blues still have a long way to go! . . . It's gonna take a lot more than a roster change for us to start winning again, let alone make the playoffs!"

"Well, ya nevva know . . . !"

I was pretty sure he was putting on the So-Con accent. Funny.

I shouted, "No!" then, with the train quieting as it slowed, lowered my voice. "You don't ever know . . . That's one of the best things about baseball."

I smiled as the train pulled into South Avenue station, and Subway Guy got up.

He turned and saw my face fully for the first time. He gave me a big, open grin.

"Now, that's something to smile about! Did you know you're glowing?"

The train jerked to a halt.

I blushed as the rider stumbled a step to the opening door, where he stopped and winked at me.

"Nice wheels. Good luck!"

I waved good-bye to him through the window. Good luck—hm.

I could swear I saw Papa Buck's statue wink at me too as I clicked by. I winked back at him: Mr. P. was putting me back in the line-up. Me and my "unexpected female trouble."

⚾ ⚾ ⚾

LLOYD PRESTON AND I SAT at his carved oak monument of a desk, leaning back and nodding our heads in agreement.

Preston leaned forward. He addressed me in a new tone, adult to adult.

"So, when can you start?"

"For you, Mr. Preston, right away. I just have to buzz the restaurant . . . 'to cancel my reservation.'"

"Mick, if you had plans . . . "

I waved off my "plans."

"No, that's OK . . . "

Mr. Preston smiled like a proud father, forgetting my stint at the Continental.

"Well, then, here, use my phone." He nudged the onyx box with its lumbering receiver toward me. As much fun as it would be to call Pops from the Bat Phone, I knew better, that I would have other chances.

"Oh, that's OK, Mr. Preston, I'll use another phone . . . " I stood up.

"As you wish, dear."

I extended my hand to Preston, who took it in both of his.

"Ah, how refreshing to have my go-getter back!"

I took three steps toward the door, then turned back and smiled at him.

"I think it's going to be good . . . for everyone. Thanks a lot, Mr. Preston."

"Call me Lloyd."

I smiled, abashed.

"OK, thanks . . . Lloyd."

Now it could start to happen. Would start to happen. Would happen.

⚾ ⚾ ⚾

JUST ONE MORE THING I had to take care of before I considered I was back: I had promised Kelly I'd explain. I left Mr. Preston's office and walked out to the reception area. She was sitting at the switch, her earpiece plugged into the Blues lifeline.

"Mornin', Kel!" She jumped to hear my voice—I had arrived before she did.

"Well, you *look* OK."

"A little better now—just met with Mr. P."

"So, what gives, Carmel?"

"I'm back!"

"You're back? Cool!—But where've ya been?"

I lowered my voice. I hoped no one would come by so I could fill her in. She really cared, she was my pal and my reputation was safe in her hands. And Mr. Preston's.

"Kel, I know I've been acting strangely. I didn't say anything, because I didn't want you to worry about me."

"Well, that kind of backfired!" I chuckled and tried not to cry. Kelly had this great talent for friendship: she could dish you the harsh truth while never causing you to doubt her love for you. In fact, the truth reinforced the love. She deserved that from me, now.

"The short version is I fraternized & fell."

"D-A?"

"Yeah. You knew?"

"I knew you had a thing for him."

"I'm not surprised. You know everything, Miss Catbird Seat."

"Well, I guess a lot. But they are educated guesses."

"It was bad, Kel. I had to ask Maggie to go with me to the clinic."

"The clinic? Oh, baby, I'm so sorry."

I started to tear up, but heard the elevator doors, so straightened up instead.

"Mick!" Blake blurted.

"Hello, Blake." I shook his hand.

"Are you back?"

"As back as I can be, just talked to Lloyd."

"Lloyd?" Kelly was laughing now.

"Yeah, he told me to call him Lloyd."

"I'd say you're back all right." Kel smiled at me and winked. Obviously our conversation would have to be put on hold.

I grabbed her hand.

"Thanks, Kel, you're the best."

⚾ ⚾ ⚾

A FEW DAYS LATER, BLAKE and Whitley sat in the Sales Office at their computers, entering ticket orders.

"He's parading her around like she's Queen Midas or something!"

"Stop whining, Whitley, we're four and oh since Mick came back."

"I thought we lost last night."

"No, Witless, it was a ninth-inning, come from behind victory: Moss singled Schlitzie and Andres in with two out. Get a clue, would you?"

It was happening.

⚾ ⚾ ⚾

UNDER MAJOR LEAGUE RULE 21, Hal Chase was finally dismissed by Giants' manager John McGraw in 1919 for "not giving one's best efforts." [†] Chase had a long-standing reputation for laying down on the job, but had been acquitted by Reds' manager Christy Mathewson of a sole earlier official charge when his teammates were suddenly unavailable to testify against him.

⚾ ⚾ ⚾

I NOW OCCUPIED MR. PRESTON's outer office formerly held by Suzanne and her emery boards. I was feeding the fax machine outside his open door and could hear him on the phone.

"I think he'll do well. He was just having trouble adjusting over here . . . He'll finish strong, and you'll be able to trade him for a bigger fish during the off-season . . . "

I listened so raptly I stopped faxing.

"I'll have my assistant—oh, you must remember Mick Carmichael . . . "

I snapped back to faxing at the sound of my name, but continued listening.

". . . she'll fax you the paperwork . . . "

I groaned at the prospect of more faxing—but—

"Nice doing business with you again, Mack. We'll look for your check tomorrow."

I stage-whispered a Marv Albert—pumped my right fist beside my head and held it there a moment: "Yeeeessss!"

My phone buzzed, and I jumped.

"Mick?"

I quickly sat at my desk and pushed the talk-back button.

"Yes . . . Lloyd."

I released the button and wiggled in my chair.

"Press release. Fax it out."

I picked the top paper off the stack sitting on my desk: "BLUES CASH IN: AKINS TO DAWGS." I realized I was gloating and superstitiously suppressed my grin.

⚾ ⚾ ⚾

I ORCHESTRATED AN EARLY MORNING press conference at Pembroke Hospital for the release of the fallen fan. There were about eleven reporters plus cameramen from various media in attendance. I stood at the podium and began.

"Ladies and gentlemen of the press." I paused to enjoy the moment: saying those words into a microphone, my amplified voice returning to my ears.

The press corps quieted to attention.

"Thank you for coming here today. The Constitution Blues felt that after all the hubbub at the time of the incident, it was important to let our #1 fan speak for himself."

I looked over at Kurt Jefferson, a 30-something father standing at the side of the room with his three children, who jostled one another excitedly. He beamed at me.

"And, since he claims he's up for dealing with you folks . . . "

A few chuckles issued from the press corps.

"I'd like to introduce Mr. Kurt Jefferson. Kurt?"

Kurt Jefferson apprehensively approached the podium, accompanied by his kids. He cleared his throat—right into the microphone.

A few more chuckles.

"Excuse me. Hi." He paused, more chuckles.

"These are my children. Ax me anything."

I interjected.

"And remember, Kurt, anything you don't want to answer, you don't have to."

Jefferson nodded, smiling at me.

Press hands shot into the air.

I nodded at Scoop Patrone, the fresh young wit from the *Daily View*, my nevva know friend from the subway.

"After the incident, there was speculation that you had jumped. Were you depressed about the team?"

"It was a acciden-t, no way did I jump."

Newsradio guy Owen Turner pursued his angle.

"Other reports stated that a Swingers fan had pushed you?"

Jefferson shook his head, laughing a little.

"Nah, well, we were a litta rowdy, but the dude dint mean nuthing."

"The railing was secure?"

The Almanack's dashing scribe and sometime pageant emcee Tom Dollyson was forever seek-and-finding reasons to support construction of a new stadium.

"Let's just say it was steadier than I was!"

Everyone cracked up.

I smiled and exchanged a glance with Scoop, motioning toward the podium with my head.

Scoop turned back to Kurt Jefferson.

"So, it was purely accidental, you were not pushed, you did not jump."

"The only jumping I'll be doing is jumping for joy when my Blues clinch the pennant!"

The media gobbled this sound bite. It was replayed ad infinitum on local broadcasts through the rest of the day: on kitchen and car radios, and living room, tavern and security desk TVs throughout the city.

⚾ ⚾ ⚾

THAT NIGHT, LIBERTY STADIUM WAS fairly full, foul pole to foul pole, even into the upper deck. Binoculars paused on the scoreboard: 4-2 Blues, bottom of the 8th. "Tonight's attendance: 41,821. The Blues and Toreadors thank you!" I leaned on the railing of the Owner's Box, holding the binoculars down now: what a beautiful, humid-sweaty crowd.

Post-game in the Press Club, I sat having a beer with Blake, Hugh, Whitley, and Scoop Patrone. Mr. Preston walked in, directly to our table.

"There's my girl! I've been looking for you!"

Whitley slitted her eyes at Blake as I greeted the boss.

"Great game, huh!"

Mr. Preston extended his hand to me, then leaned down close to whisper in my ear.

"They'd better have won after that masterful press conference."

I turned back to include everyone in the conversation.

"Kurt Jefferson's a funny guy, and he's a big fan."

"Jumping for Joy!" said Hugh. "You sure you didn't feed him that one, Mick?"

Scoop said nothing.

"Sounds like something she'd say," said Whitley.

"There's a line at tomorrow's advance ticket window," said Preston.

"She couldn't make THAT up," said Scoop.

I smiled, eyes on me. I raised my cup of beer to them.

The guys raised their cups to me. Mr. Preston patted me on the back. Whitley pseudo-toasted, sipped, and looked at me over the rim of her cup.

An hour's worth of brew later, Scoop and I headed out the Front Office door. I was puzzled by the number of post-game hangers on still hanging on, blocking our way out. Then I laughed—oh yeah!—they were in line at the Tomorrow's Game window, just like Mr. Preston had said.

My eyes fell on a fan's PM edition of the *Daily View*: "JUMPING FOR JOY—AT THE LIB?" I burst out laughing and pointed at Scoop. Scoop's brows danced: ha ha, and we took the steps two at a time down to the subway, my pumpkin-colored chariot.

ONCE IN A BLUE MOON, WHEEL OF FORTUNE & GOING ALL THE WAY

The first reference to a blue moon comes from a proverb recorded in 1528:

> *If they say the moon is blue,*
> *We must believe that it is true.*[†]

By the early 19th century, the phrase "until a blue moon" had come to mean "never." But the Maine Farmer's Almanac from that era defined a blue moon as the third full moon in a season that has four full moons; this adjustment boosted the phenomenon to "once in a blue moon." More recently a blue moon has come to mean the second full moon in a given calendar month. Over the next twenty years, there will be 15 blue moons of either type. The last one happened in May, 2007.

⚾ ⚾ ⚾

THERE WERE A FEW EMPTY Bud Light bottles and a depleted Charlie's Chips bag on the coffee table.

Paul Simon sang low from the stereo: "These are the days of miracle and wonder, don't cry, baby, don't cry, don't cry."

Carly, Maggie, Kelly and I sat on the floor watching TV. Glenn Goodall's bass outplayed the stereo.

" . . . here at beautiful Juicy Fruit Field. And, now a word from Chevy, the Heartbeat of America."

In one motion, I muted the TV, rose and turned the music up, medium loud. I swooped bottles off the table and danced to the kitchen. The others returned to their pow-wow, conversing through the commercial break: Chevy Blazers, Gotcha Razors, those and other macho crazes.

"And now the team's winning," said Carly. "It's like a dream—inside a nightmare."

"Inside a dream," said Maggie.

"You KNOW these guys are superstitious as they come!" said Kelly. "Spitting on bats? Ugh!"

I walked back in and rejoined the circle on the floor.

"Spit or no spit, we're not dreaming, we're kicking butt!"

We sat there silently for a moment. Kelly nodded at me.

"Karma. American baseball style . . . " I had finally had the chance to fill Kel in and was really happy she was over that day.

The Blues post-game show came on and we turned back to the screen. I lowered the stereo and clicked Glenn Goodall back up.

"The Blues have won another closely contested ballgame, continuing their remarkable winning streak, which now numbers . . . "

"Sweet 16 in a row!" I aped Glenn's phrasing like I wrote it. Or knew him or something.

" . . . keeping their playoff hopes alive!" he finished.

I reached out and grabbed the others, turning the powwow into a clumsy, silly, heartfelt group hug, then cackled a reminder.

"Keep your fingers crossed, my pretties!"
The others all screamed and laughed.
"AAAAAaahhhhhhhhh!!!!!"

⚾ ⚾ ⚾

NEXT EVE, BATTING PRACTICE WAS in progress at Liberty Stadium. Down on the field, *Almanack* photographer Ted Manheim aimed and shot at Doug Akins in enemy uniform greeting Bobby, who was headed down the right field line to the bullpen.

"Hey, Bobby. How goes?"

"S'goin fine, guy. Seen the Sports page lately?"

They shared a friendly chuckle, quickly followed by awkward silence.

> *And some of the bigger bears try to pretend*
> *That they came round the corner to look for a friend;*
> *And they'll try to pretend that nobody cares*
> *Whether you walk on the lines or the squares.*[†]

Doug looked down and traced the baseline with his foot, moving it side to side.

"Seen Mick around?" Doug looked up at Bobby.

Bobby looked silently at Doug a sec, then grinned.

"You bet."

"How is she?"

Bobby shrugged at Doug, shook his head, then smacked his ball into his well-worn glove.

A young Blues-capped girl at the fence waved a glove at Bobby.

"Bobby, Bobby, can I have your autograph?"

He nodded at the girl and held up his finger. First, he must finish with Doug.

"She's got a lotta balls for a chick. Fact, I may even nominate her for Comeback Player of the Year."

Doug looked puzzled.

Bobby punched Doug lightly on his right upper arm: the Dawg Patch.

"Nice threads." He walked over to the fence and pulled up the young fan's cap: a Mick look-alike. Bobby hugged her in surprise (she melted), signed her glove "Best of Luck & Love, B²" and trotted out to the bullpen, shaking his head.

The girl waved to his back.

"Good luck tonight, Bobby!!" She dashed back to her seat to show her dad Bobby's autograph.

The Lib brimmed with spirited Blues fans. Banners hung from railings throughout the park, including three different versions: "JUMPING FOR JOY," "JUMPIN 4 JOY," and "J4J." The fans were on it!

A transistor radio crackled with Glenn Goodall's voice.

"Well, it's down to the wire for the young Blues. Manager Skip Healey has handed the ball to Bobby Bahnson for Game One of this weekend's three-game series . . . "

THE FINAL JEOPARDY MUSIC PLAYED as a paper jerked through my fax machine and dropped to the floor. On screen, Alex Trebek's guests scribbled. Whitley stood by the fax, waiting to feed the next sheet.

I straightened papers on my desk and teased Whitley.

"This is what's known as 'down to the wire,' Whitley. What is: we have to win all three games this weekend, or it's 'next year.'"

"No kidding, Mick!"

I laughed.

Whitley shook her head.

"There's no way I could live through another season like this. I'm quitting if we don't get into the playoffs." A season like this? There would be no other.

"Jumping ship already! That's great for team karma, Whitley."

> *To become a popular religion, it is only necessary*
> *for a superstition to enslave a philosophy.*[†]

"Team kar-ma?" Whitley exhaled, exasperated—yet another baseball concept she must try to comprehend. She looked at me, and I rubbed my right fingertips against my thumb.

"That indiscernible essence which binds a team and determines its fate . . . "

Whitley fed another paper into the fax and looked at the TV, tuning me out.

The opening sequence of "Wheel of Fortune" scrolled on the screen, as I continued.

" . . . vaguely related to the scales of justice . . . "

Charlie O'Donnell on voice-over, introduced " . . . the host of Wheel of Fortune, Pat Sajak!"

I looked over and saw Whitley wasn't listening. I raised my voice, feigning aggravation.

" . . . or I guess YOU might relate it to the 'Wheel of Fortune'!"

I spun in my chair as I spoke, reached over and flipped the channel.

Whistling and cheering sang from the TV.

"Hey! I was watching that!" said Whitley.

"Why don't you watch a few innings tonight, Whitley? Just your watching might help us win. Ever think about that?"

Whitley considered my pitch for a minute, then pulled a chair to the fax machine, sat down and looked at the TV.

On screen, Bobby took the mound and threw a warm-up, hard.

I nodded in approval at the TV, fixing a willful gaze on Bobby as he threw again.

"We can do it, Whitley. Watch us do it."

> *Nothing is so contagious as enthusiasm. It is the real allegory of the tale of Orpheus; it moves stones and charms brutes. It is the genius of sincerity and truth accomplishes no victories without it.*[†]

Post-game, the Blue Moon taproom was packed and buzzing like neon. Blues game-timers gathered in the back booth. A young Blue Belle, a 20-ish Malibu Barbie-blonde, squeezed in with the veterans.

"Did you see Bobby strike his ass out?" shouted a groundcrew guy over Springsteen on the juke box with *his* big baseball player.

"The first time was the best," said everyone's favorite usherette Roe Duffy. "It's always fun to see them stand there and watch the ball go by!"

Everyone laughed.

"I wonder what the report on his knee is?" said the young Belle.

"I saw the replay," said Debbie. "Chubby Checker couldn't have done it better."

"Wasn't it just a stall tactic so that their reliever could have more time to warm up?" Malibu Belle was on the case: she had already learned about relievers' 8-pitch limit once they've taken the mound.

"I heard he's a good actor," said Roe.

A Blues fan, an early 20s, clean cut guy feeling his post-game flush, leaned over from the table behind young Malibu.

"The stall certainly didn't pay off."

The others at the table raised their glasses.

"Yaaaaay, team!" Others whistled.

The rookie Belle smiled at the fan.

He leaned in right close to her ear.

"We're going all the way." The nerve of the guy!

"Excuuuuse me?"

The others at the table saw she was blushing confused, and kidded her as only they could.

"All the way! All the way! All the way!"

The new Belle and the fan laughed and raised their glasses as the chant was taken up by everyone in the bar.

"All the way!! All the way!!"

As the bar quieted back down, the fan leaned back to the Belle.

"Maybe I shouldn't've said that. We should keep cool, we still have two more games to win."

⚾ ⚾ ⚾

SATURDAY, THE WEATHER WAS GAME-PERFECT: bright, sunny and coolish. I walked the route to the Continental, stopping at the newsstand to check the headlines: "BAHNSON BURNER" was the *Daily View*'s tag. *The Almanack* read "TWO ARE BETTER THAN WON."

Though Gunner *was* throwing that night, wasn't that pushing it a little, boys?

I stopped at the diner door and looked across the street at the proud white steeple of Trinity Church. Its bells chimed noon. I entered the Continental and headed to the back table.

Pops looked up from his crossword.

"'Ere she is!"

"Just two more! . . . " I hugged him hello. "And you're going tomorrow!"

His eyes grew big.

"Whaddaya mean, Mick, it's sold out fer weeks!" Pops was glad that big shot Lloyd Preston was smart enough to take me back, but he hadn't yet grasped I had any so-called pull. Pandora and I, we were still hoping.

"Let's just say . . . ya gotta know sumbuddy . . . "

Pops grinned at me, thrilled, but his face quickly turned gray.

"Whatsamatta now?" I asked, kidding him in my best So-Con accent.

Pops hesitated.

"If they lose tonight, then tomorra never comes . . . "

I scolded him, arms akimbo.

"We're not going to lose, kid!"

We shared a laugh, then I patted his arm.

"I'll meet you here tomorrow, same Bat Time . . . "

" . . . same Bat Channel!" Pops echoed.

"And I'll personally walk you through the 'complicated' Courtesy Gate routine so you'll start coming down next year."

I turned to leave, and Pops yelled after me.

"Here! Take this."

Pops handed me his *Daily View*.

I smiled at him, and he yelled after me once more as he watched me hurry out.

"I'd give ya both, but I'm not done with this one yet . . . Goin' to my nephew's tonight . . . he's got the cable! . . . Have fun . . . and I'll see ya tomorra!"

He turned back to his paper.

"The bums."

⚾ ⚾ ⚾

THE HANDS ON THE SALES Office clock were straight up, 12 o'clock. Kelly and I sorted playoff ticket orders post-game, our beer cups nestled twixt stacks of ticket boxes.

"Hi, excuse me."

Kel and I looked up in unison. There stood Liz.

"Do you know where the Ladies' Room is? They've remodeled since I was here last."

I looked at her. She was sporting an oversized gold 13 around her neck.

"We have made some changes . . . "

Kelly grinned and held up two fingers at her: a peace sign, a victory V, 2 wins.

"We're playing clutch baseball since you were here."

I turned back to the tickets, stifling a giggle.

"You must be excited," said Liz.

Kelly turned back to her work, throwing her thumb over her shoulder.

"The john's that way."

Liz walked toward the bathroom.

Kelly and I stared at each other a sec, then she raised her beer to me. My eyes welled, and I turned away from her. She grabbed me.

"Don't be getting all girly on me now, Carmel, or we'll never get out of here!"

We laughed and I dabbed my eyes. We regrouped as Liz came back through.

I sipped my beer.

"Well, good luck in the playoffs." Liz walked out.

I looked at Kelly.

"Think she knows?"

Kelly considered my question a moment, then shook her head.

"Not much—she wished us good luck."

THE CHURCH OF BASEBALL, TEAM KARMA & CHAMPIONSHIP PIE

*. . . battering the gates of heaven
with storms of prayer. †*

Tommy Lasorda noticed opposing manager John McNamara one Sunday morning light a candle after Mass, so he lit one too.†

With a secure lead into the late innings of that afternoon's Reds-Dodgers contest, McNamara yelled over to Lasorda.

"I lit a candle! I lit a candle!"

But Tommy didn't worry. The Dodgers rallied in the last of the ninth to win, and Tommy yelled back.

"I blew yours out! I blew yours out!"

TRINITY CHURCH WAS PIN-DROP QUIET. Pops and I lit votive candles in the rear vestibule. Carly stood to the side waiting, then quickly lit a votive too as we turned to leave. She exited behind me and Pops through the heavy, carved doors, and we started down Second Street.

"Oldest place of worship in the city, the real Sons of Liberty knelt there, had to do it." I was relieved to have taken care of that final curse-lifting chore. Gotta light a candle!

I was convinced that certain actions had to be taken, steps fulfilled, in order that the world could set itself right again. The team could now take the pennant.

"You sure I didn't jinx it, Mick, being Jewish and all?" Carly kidded me, then added, perhaps a bit more seriously, "I wasn't sure whether to light a candle or not!"

"I don't think God cares what religion anyone is," I said.

"I know some people who worship at the ballpark," Carly joked.

"Can you imagine?" said Pops. We all laughed.

I grabbed Carly's and Pops's arms. We walked, quicker now, arm-in-arm-in-arm past the Continental, descended the steps of the 2nd Street El stop and waited on the platform. A few minutes passed.

Pops looked up from his *Daily View* and turned to me.

"So, when's the last time you been ta Mass, kid?"

"I say my prayers, Pops."

The El pulled into the station, its screechy brakes ending the conversation. We embarked, then transferred to the Centre Street Line downtown, and tumbled through the turnstiles at Liberty Stadium station with a slew of other early-birds in their dress Blues. (More people come earlier when it's a practical playoff.)

I saluted Papa Buck on our way into the park. I swear he winked back.

⚾ ⚾ ⚾

BINOCULARS SCANNED THE FRESHLY-LINED ASTROTURF, the back of the batting cage, and the Owner's Box railing, where I sat inspecting the proceedings.

Carly handed the binoculars to Pops.

"Look, there she is!"

Pops fumbled with the binoculars, catching a fleeting glimpse as I ascended the stairs of the box.

"That's our girl!"

Pops and Carly settled in behind homeplate, taking in the pregame atmosphere, looking at the field as they talked. It was much bigger than it looked on TV.

"So when's the last time you came to a Blues game?" Carly asked Pops.

"Never even been ta this park. Must be over twenty years . . . Looks like it was worth the wait!"

"Mick definitely hooked us up for this one. Great dogs, huh?" Carly took another bite from her half-eaten wiener. The fresh ones at the ballpark actually do snap against your teeth and lips—not so in the later innings.

"As long as the beer's cold . . . " Pops took a sip and nodded. "These bums better come through." (In case you're worried, Pops was absolved of violating the 2nd inning beer rule, because he didn't know it. Some people think sex ed works like that.)

⚾ ⚾ ⚾

IN THE BLUES CLUBHOUSE, MANAGER Skip Healey addressed his warriors in preparation for their final battle. To get to the next level, you must fight as though it is your last shot, for your last breath, because unless you win this one, it IS your final battle.

"We've been working toward this all season, champs, and, Lord knows, we've been through a lot."

"Skip," Mark Ridley interrupted.

Healey raised his eyebrow at Mark.

" . . . if you don't mind, I'd like to offer a prayer."

Healey shrugged then nodded at Mark.

"It IS Sunday." Healey bowed his head.

The players all bowed their heads: Ridley's praying?

"Oh, Mighty Lord, please help us to do our best today. Forgive us our errors of the past . . . and keep us from them in the future . . . "

"Amen?" Bobby said, eyeballing Skip, who had raised his head.

"Amen," said Mark and Skip together.

Everyone else answered "Amen," except Jack Black, who yelled.

"AAAAAAA-MEN!"

He was giving them all the finger: the one which he had nearly lost, now scarred over.

Everyone busted up. They were ready.

⚾ ⚾ ⚾

LLOYD PRESTON AND I NODDED to each other, a silent Amen, as we met in the hallway outside our offices. We could hear the sellout crowd finishing the Anthem.

". . . and the home—of the—brrrraave!"

We watched the game from the Owner's Box. I bit my lip. Preston swigged his Mylanta. The afternoon's play had so far been patchy. The Blues may have said their prayers, but perhaps had forgotten to spit on their bats.

"Damn! They get ahead, they give up a bunch of runs. What IS this?"

I patted his hand, stiff-upper-lipping it for him.

"Lloyd, calm down. It's baseball. You remember." I laughed at my own joke.

Preston reprimanded me with a glare. Making the playoffs meant a lot of money.

I gestured to the field.

"It's only the sixth."

"That's what's getting me! Pretty soon there won't be any pitchers to finish the game. These boys are tired."

"It's been a long one," I had to agree.

"God help us," said Preston. Candles and prayers: can they, do they really work?

This suspense is terrible. I hope it will last.[†]

When your team's season is on the last day of the season line, freaking out comes as naturally as calling on The Divine.

"I'm gonna havva heart attack hee-yah!" Pops yelled. "Heaven help me!"

After checking that Pops was actually OK, Carly chimed in.

"C'mon, ya bums! Pops is gonna have a heart attack! . . . And so am I!"

Jack Black approached the batter's box. The Constitution Blues fans cheered wildly.

"Jack it, Black! Go, Jack!"

Jack stood in and the fans grew quiet, holding their breath as one. He pointed his left foot, marked an X on the plate with his Kentucky Slugger, and, feet parallel, wiggled his hips for the swing. Fore!

He fried that first pitch over the left field fence to put the Blues up by two.

Blake and Whitley sat at the end of Press Row, trying not to cheer. (Showing any emotion, let alone rooting in the Press Box, is practically illegal.)

"A double-switch?" Whitley said.

"Right," said Blake, eyes sticking with the action. "They bring in someone who can hit at the same time they put in a new reliever, inserting the hitter into the spot in the batting line-up formerly held by the pitcher who got yanked. Got that?"

Whitley tilted her head to one side, like the RCA dog listening for His Master's Voice. She closed one eye briefly, then straightened her head and looked at Blake.

"That means . . . next inning . . . " Whitley's eyes got big.

Blake nodded.

"Whitley, there may be hope for you yet!"

She had been waiting for the right time to spring her latest baseball knowledge on him.

"Friday night," she said, "Mick was explaining to me about team karma."

"Yeah?" Blake said, half-interested, half is-this-necessary.

"It's like the Wheel of Fortune." Whitley, with great self-satisfaction, looked back out at the field.

Blake inhaled his Press Box emotions.

Doug Akins, with two on and two out for the Bulldawgs, stepped into the on-deck circle swinging a weighted bat.

"Ya bum, Akins! Howz yer knee?" Pops yelled from his best-seat-in-the-house seat behind home plate.

Doug looked up in the bleachers in the direction of the shouter.

Pops looked down the first base line toward the Blues bullpen.

Bobby came swinging through the door, into a saloon of 60,000 screaming Blues fans. The "one who saves" in baseball is called a reliever. He brings us relief from the edge of our seats, our life, our pain, our death by curveball.

The hometown fans, they thought they had the deep background on this match-up: former Triple-A farmboy teammates, best friends, now lookee here.

"Ya wimp! Strike him out, Bobby!!"

Doug turned back to the field and saw Bobby stalking toward the mound, raising his old glove to the crowd—and looking at him as a hawk would a field mouse. Relievers can redeem infinite earlier mistakes of their teammates by sheer concentration alone. Like Jesus taking on our sins. *That* was some concentration of power.

"C'mon, Bobby! Do it, PLEAEASE!" Carly's shout rode the crowd's sound past the plate, out to the mound.

Bobby burned one warm-up down the pike—SMACK! into Moss Thorne's mitt—and nodded to the ump.

It's a funny thing, but you can recognize a familiar voice yelling your name if you're out on the field in a packed baseball house.

Carly swore Bobby heard her.

He did, but they never said anything.

Later, it was just another part of what happened.

Doug stepped in.

> *His honour rooted in dishonour stood,*
> *And faith unfaithful kept him falsely true.*[†]

I sat silently with my hands clasped in my lap, power eyes on Bobby, Mr. Preston stone-faced beside me. I yelled.

"No batta, no batta, no batttterrrr!"

Preston shook his head at me and lifted his binoculars.

Bobby went into his wind up.

"Here you go, Doug. Here's a beachball for you."

Doug fouled off Bobby's first pitch.

The crowd cheered, 0-1, then quieted for Bobby's next pitch. Then a few people started to whistle, the clapping gathered steam.

> *Fair is foul, and foul is fair;*
> *Hover through the fog and filthy air.*[†]

Bobby threw again, and Doug hit a long ball—just foul of the yellow net in right.

"Oooo . . . " Now the crowd was on its 0-2 feet, clapping and stomping. Bobby was hot.

"BAHN-SON!!" clap clap, "BAHN-SON!!" clap clap! Pops yelled, "Go, Bob!"

Carly looked up towards the Owner's Box, then back at Bobby. "Do it, Bobby!!!"

Up in the Owner's Box, Mr. Preston and I drew our breath with the full house.

Bobby threw from the stretch, a two-strike fastball down the middle.

Doug swung, nothing but air. Moss jumped up and raised the ball.

The Blues mobbed Bobby on the mound, and the Lib broke into a pandemonium.

Mr. Preston and I embraced. The neon bell in center flashed, and the EAST CHAMPIONSHIP banner unfurled like magic down the left field wall.

"We did it, Mick." *We*, yes, I was part of the team—and I had some good teammates.

"Bobby's not bad—for a ballplayer." My eyes crested as I smiled at him.

The phone rang.

"East Champion Constitution Blues, Owner's Box." Preston laughed. I hung up.

"They want you downstairs."

"You'll come with me, of course."

I took Mr. Preston's right hand for a shake, then leaned in and put my left arm around him.

"I'm right behind you," I said with a hug. "I just have to stop in my office a minute." Preston stepped back and looked at me. I saw my bonus in his eyes.

"Hurry up," he said. "We've got to discuss playoff strategy."
We laughed at his new-found—feminism?

⚾ ⚾ ⚾

I SAT AT MY DESK and made the call.

"Beauty and timelessness . . . You're definitely coming down to the playoffs."

"Too bad Dad wasn't here to see the bums pull it off," said Uncle Pat.

"Oh, he was here . . . " Fact, he sat with Carly, I thought.

"I'll call you tomorrow—Mr. P's expecting me downstairs. Bye!"

I rode the elevator down to the clubhouse. I danced around, jamming to the song in my head: We Are The Champions? Wow! That first night in the Blue Belles lockerroom seemed so long ago.

The elevator landed, and I danced off—right into Doug.

"Oh!"

"Mary K, I've been looking all over for you."

Game face.

"You have?"

He held out a white envelope.

"I wanted to give this to you."

I looked at the envelope, looked at him.

"Liz doesn't know, does she?"

"No. Nobody knows."

I considered him a moment, then turned to leave.

"Here, take this."

"No, thanks."

I started to walk.

Doug called after me again.

"But I told you I would pay you back."

He said pay like pie.

I turned around and looked at him once more.

"That at bat settled it for me. Excuse me." Outta here.

I turned on my heel and resisted running toward the Constitution Blues clubhouse. I reached the door and tugged its handle. Waves of laughter and celebration flowed over me as I walked in, right hand aloft with the Victory V.

The first face I saw was Kelly's, Kel flashing the V back at me. Hugh rushed up and handed me a Bud. The Blue Sea parted as I walked up the aisle between the lockers to where Lloyd Preston stood looking at me, so happy. Even Whitley was clapping.

Of course we went all the way.

And Bobby gave me his glove.

⚾ ⚾ ⚾

IN A CONSTITUTION PHOTOGRAPHY STUDIO, Ted Manheim focused on my hand with its World Series ring gripping the top of a baseball bat.

There was a pop! And then a flash went off.

Next came Bobby's hand with its ring, grabbing my hand: Pop! Flash.

Mark's ring hand grabbed Bobby's: Pop! Flash.

Tommy's hand grabbed Mark's: Pop! Flash.

Jack's scarred finger next to his ring: Pop! Flash.

All hands fly up as in a pregame cheer.

⚾ ⚾ ⚾

In a backyard somewhere in America,
children's hands fly up.

"Go, team!"

A wifflebat falls to the freshly mown lawn.

THE POST-GAME SHOW:
LIFTING THE CURSE

*Life does not imitate the World Series,
and it doesn't begin on Opening Day.[†]*

When your home team wins, it's revolutionary, a city-wide ecumenical celebration, a unifying spirit: we are REDEEMED! The League Championship Series and World Series are like Holy Days of Obligation: no one misses an inning. Temporarily, the city's ills, aches and pains are forgotten. Everyone is a brother or sister in a team cap. Old neighbors reminisce about the last time *we* won. New neighbors are no longer strangers but fellow celebrants. Every kid MUST have an UTLEY jersey, dusty with afternoons of sweating the final out, unwashed, because "it could break the spell, Mom."

But this was the Hollywood version of the legend. I never returned to the team and the curse persisted.

An Indonesian superstition holds that one should change one's name after a serious illness or misfortune to confuse the bad spirit so it will be unable to recognize and pursue you.[†]

I moved to MetroCity and changed my name. Bobby eventually got his ring—wearing a different uniform. Kelly kept track of me and remained my steadfast friend through it all.

In a blue moon moment, April 2007, I bumped into Mr. Preston at a Constitution literary event. He was surprised to hear how long it had been since I had worked for him and asked me what I had been up to. I handed him my blurb card for this story: THE CONSTITUTION BLUES: A Tale of Sex, Karma and a Pox on the Church of Baseball. He chuckled nervously. I decided it was time to lift the curse and visited his new cathedral Fourth of July weekend. We beat the Metros on the last day of the season to clinch the division. Then the following year we won the Series. Sometimes you have to show up before God can.

"World Champions . . .
World Fucking Champions!"

—Chase Utley—
Phillies Second Baseman
October 31, 2008

APPENDIX

R.I.P:
BASEBALL LEGENDS

Hugh Alexander	Thacher Longstreth
Marge Annan	John Marzano
Rich Ashburn	Maje McDonnell
Rich Bruner	Tug McGraw
Joe Burgoyne, Jr.	Chollie McNamara
Pat Cassidy	John McSherry
Pete Cera	Foster Mears
Claire Clay	Bill Montgomery
Tom Connor	Bruce Montgomery
Bo Diaz	June Manuel
Ted DiMuzio	Jim O'Brien
Carmen DiNovi	Paul Owens
Jackie Donnelly	Paul Richardson
Mark Drucker	Joan Rosney
Eddie Ferenz	Kevin J. Smith
Eric Gregg	Bill Stratton
Frank Griffin	Hattie Stratton
Jack Halpin	Frank Sullivan
Jeffery Hudson	Tom Taglialatela
Tom Hudson	Tom Tumelty
Yallie Hudson	Brenda Vinci
Johanna Ilens	John Vukovich
Harry Kalas	Bob Vetrone
Teddy Kessler	Lee Weyer
Helen Krise	The Vet
Bill Leahy	The Curse

†Color Commentary:
The Quotes

Page 54
Major League Rule 21—*Baseball Blue Book*

Page 58
The Seventh Commandment—*The Bible v Wicked King James Bible, 1631*

4TH

Page 59
It is a public scandal that gives offense —*Moliere, Tartuffe*

Page 70
Major League Rule 34 —*Baseball Blue Book*

Page 75
I used to be Snow White, but I drifted —*The Wit and Wisdom of Mae West*

Page 78
Insurance v. going to Hell—*Rob Brezny's Free Will Astrology, 3/19/02*

Page 79
Thought must be divided against itself —*Aldous Huxley, Do What You Will*

Page 80
Man with Experience never at mercy —*Pentecostal saying*

5TH

Page 88
Tears from the depth of divine despair—*Tennyson, The Princess*

Page 94
oyako-shinju —*www.japanpsychiatrist.com/Abstracts/Shinju.html*

Page 94
mizuko —*http://en.wikipedia.org/wiki/Mizuko_kuyō*

Page 95
For why should my freedom be determined by someone else's conscience — *1 Corinthians 10:29*

Page 95
People tend to avoid risk —*Kahneman and Tversky*

Page 96
Odds of murdering a genius—*Morris Kline, Math for the Nonmathematician*

Page 97
The heart has its reasons—*Blaise Pascal, Pensées sur la religion*

6TH

Page 101
Superstition that virginity=virtue—*Voltaire, Leningrad Notebook*

Page 103
The devil made me do it—*Flip Wilson*

Page 106
Cardinal Ratzinger's Moral Relativism—*America Magazine, 3/6/99*

Page 107
Greatest injury basing morals on myth—*Viscount Samuel, Romanes Lecture, 1947*

7TH

Page 122
Abortion patients' decision-making—*Sarah Cirese, Quest: A Search for Self*

Page 124
Alcohol v drug abuse: Alcohol abuse, responsible for 80,000 to 100,000 deaths per year in the U.S. and a contributing factor in 100,000 others, is by a variety of measures considerably more costly than drug abuse.—*John Allen Paulos, Innumeracy*

Page 124
Crab Nebula: "The supernova explosion that created the Crab was seen on about July 4 1054 AD. It was recorded by Chinese astronomers and perhaps others."—*www.astro.nineplanets.org/twn/n1952x.html*

10TH

Page 160
If they say the moon is blue—*www.infoplease.com/spot/bluemoon1.html*

Page 162
And some of the bigger bears pretend—*AA Milne, Lines and Squares*

Page 164
To become a popular religion—*William Ralph Inge, Outspoken Essays*

Page 165
Nothing is so contagious as enthusiasm—*Baron Edward Bulwer-Lytton*

11TH

Page 169
Battering the gates of heaven—*Tennyson, St. Simeon Stylites*

Page 169
Votive candle story—*Tommy Lasorda, Late Night w/D. Letterman*

Page 173
This suspense is terrible—*Oscar Wilde, The Importance of Being Earnest*

Page 175
His honour rooted in dishonour stood—*Tennyson, Idylls of the King: Lancelot & Elaine*

Page 175
Fair is foul, and foul is fair—*Shakespeare, That Scottish Play*

POST-GAME SHOW

Page 180
Life does not imitate the World Series—*Stephen Jay Gould, The New York Times*

Page 180
Indonesian Superstition re name change—*Dunkling, First Names First*

BIBLIOGRAPHY

America Magazine, "Ratzinger cites 'need for moral absolutes,'"
6 Mar. 99: 5.

Asimov, Isaac. *Words from the Myths.* New York: Houghton Mifflin
Harcourt, 1962.

Baseball Blue Book. St. Petersburg, Florida, 1984.

Berger, Douglas, M.D. and Yoshitomo Takahashi, M.D. "Cultural
Dynamics and the Unconscious Suicide in Japan," *Suicide and the
Unconscious.* Leenaars A. and Lester D. (Eds.), Northvale: Jason
Aronson, 1996.

Bulwer-Lytton, Edward G. *The Last Days Of Pompeii.* Little,
Brown, and Company, 1893.

Burke, Edmund. *Present State of the Nation, Observations on a late
publication.* 1769.

Burke, Edmund. *Reflections on the Revolution in France.* 1790.

Campbell, Joseph and Bill Moyers. *The Power of Myth.* New York:
Broadway Books, 1988.

Cirese, Sarah. *Quest: A Search For Self.* New York: Holt, Rinehart
and Winston, 1977.

Dunkling. Leslie Alan. *First Names First.* Worthing, West Sussex,
United Kingdom: Littlehampton Book Services, 1977.

Franklin, Benjamin. *Poor Richard's Almanack.* Philadelphia, 1743.

Giego, Diana, Lou Kilzer and Norman Udevitz. "The Truth
About Missing Kids," *The Denver Post,* March and December,
1985. (1986 Pulitzer Prize for Public Service)

Huxley, Aldous. *Do What You Will.* New York: Doubleday, Doran
& Company, 1929.

Inge, William Ralph. *Outspoken Essays.* 1919.

Jefferson, Thomas. *Letter to Richard Rush, October 20, 1820.*
(L&B.15.283)

Kahneman, Daniel and Amos Tversky. "Prospect Theory: An Analysis of Decision under Risk." *Econometrica* 47 1979, 263-291.

Kline, Morris. *Mathematics for the Nonmathematician.* Mineola, New York: Dover Publications, Inc., 1985.

Maguire, Daniel, *Sacred Choices: Right to Contraception and Abortion in World Religions*, Augsburg Fortress Press, 2001

Mazer, Bill. *Bill Mazer's Amazin' Baseball Book: 150 Years of Tales and Trivia from Baseball's Earliest Beginnings Down to the Present Day.* New York: Zebra Books, 1990.

Melville, Herman. "Hawthorne and His Mosses." *The Literary World* (Aug. 17-24, 1850)

Milne, A.A. "Lines and Squares." *When We Were Very Young.* London: Methuen & Co., 1924.

Moliere. *Tartuffe* (play), 1670.

Page Brookes, Anne. "Mizuko Kuyō and Japanese Buddhism," *Japanese Journal of Religious Studies* 8 (3-4) 1981, 119-47.

Pascal, Blaise. *Pensées de M. Pascal sur la religion, et sur quelques autres sujets* ("Thoughts of M. Pascal on religion, and on some other subjects"). 1670.

Paulos, John Allen. *Innumeracy: Mathematical Illiteracy and Its Consequences.* New York: Hill and Wang, 2001.

Rickey, Branch. "Luck is the residue of design." Lecture title, 1950.

Viscount Samuel. "Creative Man." *Romanes Lecture 1947.* Oxford: Clarendon Press, 1947.

Star, Alexander. "Life's Work: Questions for Stephen Jay Gould." *New York Times Magazine*, June 2, 2002.

Tennyson, Alfred Lord. "Lancelot and Elaine." *Idylls of the King*, 1859.

Tennyson, Alfred Lord. *In Memoriam A.H.H.*, 1849.

Tennyson, Alfred Lord. *The Princess*, 1847.

Tennyson, Alfred Lord. *St Simeon Stylites*, 1842.

Travers, P.L. *Mary Poppins.* London: HarperCollins, 1934.

Twain, Mark. "Pudd'nhead Wilson's New Calendar" (Chapter 51 epigraph), *Following the Equator*, 1897.

Voltaire (François-Marie Arouet). *Leningrad Notebook (Le Sottisier)*. c. 1750 (posthumously published).

Voltaire (François-Marie Arouet). The *Dictionnaire philosophique* (Philosophical Dictionary). 1764.

West, Mae. *I'm No Angel* (screenplay), 1933.

Wilde, Oscar. *The Ballad of Reading Gaol*, 1899.

Wilde, Oscar. *The Importance of Being Earnest* (play), 1895.

Wilhelm, Joseph. "Superstition." *The Catholic Encyclopedia*. Vol. 14. New York: Robert Appleton Company, 1912. 17 Mar. 2010 *http://www.newadvent.org/cathen/14339a.htm*.

Wilson, Flip. *The Flip Wilson Show*, September 17, 1970-June 27, 1974.

Zolecki, Todd. "A Cry for Help." *The Philadelphia Inquirer*, July 8, 2006.

POST-GAME SHOW
by Ronnie Norpel

What you want
You usually get
A gold Longines wristwatch
Or a nice sweater set

Today I have something
Better yet
I have to give you thanks
For being my guest

You're a real good hitter
I like your style
(And—heh, heh—you really
Drive those young girls wild!)

Who taught you that
Batting stance
How to play this
Game of chance

How old were you
When you first played
When did you know
You had it made

Tell me all about it
That sweet clean sweep
You off your feet
That diving leap

Coming up with
The big clutch hit
Knowing how to
Never quit

Your all-time best catch
Cheers in the stands
Meeting your match
Greeting the fans

You really are
A Consummate Pro
That's all for today
We have to go

CPSIA information can be obtained
at www.ICGtesting.com
Printed in the USA
FFHW022349030419
51385418-56879FF